# ALSO BY APRIL DÁVILA

*142 Ostriches*

"If you want to learn how to meditate and use it to deepen your writing, this simple, knowledgeable, and encouraging book can show you how."
—**Jack Kornfield**, *New York Times* bestselling author

"I strongly recommend to beginning writers and seasoned professionals alike Dávila's lessons on how the practice of mindfulness meditation and Buddhist wisdom can enhance one's creativity. *Sit Write Here* is filled with reader-friendly instruction worthy of our trust."
—**Charles Johnson**, National Book Award–winning author of *Middle Passage* and *The Way of the Writer*

"The tool kit every writer needs to stay focused and do their best work."
—**Zibby Owens**, author, publisher, and podcast host

"I would have killed for a book like this when I was starting out. Dávila gets the balance of craft and consciousness exactly right and shows that noticing lies is at the heart of it all. Compassionate and wise, yet filled with practical techniques, tips, and tricks, *Sit Write Here* is a marvelous work, destined to live on every writer's shelf, dog-eared and often returned to."
—**Mark Sarvas**, award-winning novelist

"Dávila guides writers through the ups and downs of the journey of the writing process, pointing them to the most essential—that which lies within."
—**Ofosu Jones-Quartey (Born I)**, author of *Lyrical Dharma*

"Wise, grounding, and deeply encouraging, *Sit Write Here* offers mindfulness practices that will profoundly alter the way you approach the page. Anyone seeking greater peace, clarity, and confidence in their writing will find true guidance here."
—**Debra Landwehr Engle**, author of
*The Writer's Miracle Method*

"Dávila approaches writing as an ongoing practice of attention, and strengthens a writer's ability to finish what they start. *Sit Write Here* is a steady companion you'll return to again and again throughout your writing life."
—**Jennie Nash**, founder and CEO of Author Accelerator

"A masterful and necessary guide showing writers that the path to a powerful, consistent practice in our hyper-distracted world is found in stillness . . . The essential tool kit for every author seeking to move from mental chaos to creative flow. I will be using and recommending it!"
—**Faith Adiele**, award-winning author of *Meeting Faith*

"*Sit Write Here* makes a clear and compelling case for how meditation and mindfulness practice can help writers do their best work."
—**Brad Listi**, bestselling author and host of *Otherppl*

"A generous and grounding book for writers and mindfulness practitioners alike, coming from April's lived wisdom both as a writer and as a meditator. I was personally inspired to begin writing again after reading this."
—**Celeste Young**, Theravadin Buddhist
mindfulness and Dharma teacher

# SIT WRITE HERE

6 MINDFULNESS PRACTICES

TO HELP YOU

WRITE MORE AND SUFFER LESS

## APRIL DÁVILA

ST. MARTIN'S
ESSENTIALS
NEW YORK

First published in the United States by St. Martin's Essentials,
an imprint of St. Martin's Publishing Group

*EU Representative:* Macmillan Publishers Ireland Ltd, 1st Floor, The Liffey
Trust Centre, 117–126 Sheriff Street Upper, Dublin 1, D01 YC43



www.stmartins.com

Designed by Steven Seighman
Interior art by Michele Collier

The Library of Congress Cataloging-in-Publication Data
is available upon request.

ISBN 978-1-250-42523-2 (trade paperback)
ISBN 978-1-250-42524-9 (ebook)



Our books may be purchased in bulk for specialty retail/wholesale, literacy,
corporate/premium, educational, and subscription box use. Please contact
MacmillanSpecialMarkets@macmillan.com.

First Edition: 2026

10 9 8 7 6 5 4 3 2 1

*For Daniel*
*my fellow traveler on the path*

# CONTENTS

# A NOTE FROM THE AUTHOR

Focus has become a rare commodity. We live in a world that is designed to pull our attention in a thousand directions with an endless churn of social media, notifications, and algorithmic noise that leaves us depleted and unmoored. Writing, more than almost anything else, asks for the opposite: stillness, presence, a mind that can rest in one place long enough to follow a thread where it leads. That's no longer our default state. If you're feeling that, you're not alone, and it's not your fault, but it is in your power to change it. In many ways, engaging in activities that require deep thought has become a radical act. It's true in all aspects of our lives, but for writing in particular, and if you've picked up this book, it's highly likely that you are, or long to be, a writer.

You probably have ideas that bang around inside your skull while you're driving your car or washing the dishes. You're well-versed in what it's like to struggle with distractions. Maybe you're familiar with the pressure of writer's block or the unruly voices of inner critics that seem intent on shutting you down before you even get started. Perhaps you've amassed a collection of notes scribbled on scraps of paper and you steal time whenever you can to try to get words on the page. You do all this with the intention of putting your work out into the world, where inevitably someone (somewhere) will not appreciate it. Rejection, criticism, and disappointment are part of being a writer. If you want to stay in this game, you have to learn to deal with those, too.

All of which is to say: Writing can be hard.

Writing well can be even harder. In my experience, writing only gets more challenging as you get better at it. Before I cared about diction, imagery, and precision, I could slap together a few thousand words on instinct and call it a story. These days, I take the time to home in on and whittle away at ideas until the words on the page accurately represent what I'm trying to say. It's work that requires deep focus. It's hard. And I love it.

I can't promise to make writing easier, but in these pages I've accumulated the insights and practices that have helped me to write more and suffer less, because even if you don't believe me just yet, you *can* do hard things without all the agonizing. It took me a long time to untangle this pain and suffering, and I owe my moment of revelation to a big pile of onions. Come with me on a little jaunt back in time, and I'll tell you about the day that changed everything for me.

## PAIN AND SUFFERING

On my first extended meditation retreat, in 2009, the instructor gave a talk about how mindfulness can help us discern the difference between pain and suffering. I was *not* getting it. Pain and suffering. One follows the other like day follows night. To be in pain is to suffer. I suffer when I'm in pain. End of story.

After the talk, I walked down the hill to the kitchen for my work duty. At this retreat, every attendee had a job to do and I had volunteered to help chop veggies for the dinner meal. I strolled into the kitchen to join my fellow yogis as the head cook poured out a box of onions and told us to start dicing.

I dutifully set to chopping. I wasn't even done cutting the first onion when my eyes began to sting. By the second onion, tears were streaming down my face. I sniffed and heard the woman next to me do the same. The man on the other side of the table turned away, wiping his eyes with the inside of his sleeve. Pretty soon I could hardly see for the tears. My eyes were burning. The discomfort quickly edged into pain, yet I found myself giggling at the absurdity of us, crying over those onions.

The other veggie choppers began to chuckle as well. We stood there, alternately laughing with tears streaming down our faces and turning away to try to catch our breath, blink away the sting, and compose ourselves, with no success.

Had I been in a different, less mindful state, I might have spun up some story about how I'm no good at chopping onions. My tears could have been used as confirmation that I was not made for that job, it was too hard, too painful. I might have quit. Instead, I carried on tittering with my fellow onion choppers as we tried to dice onions we could barely see. Thankfully (since I'd been meditating for several days straight), I was able to notice what was happening: I was in pain, yet I was *not* suffering. I was having fun.

I think about those onions a lot.

If I were a more mystically minded person, I might say that

the universe conspired in that moment to help me understand a lesson I was struggling to grasp. But I believe there are countless opportunities for understanding that exist all around us all the time. It's where you choose to put your attention that determines the lessons you learn.

This book is based in science. I will cite studies and point you toward research that supports everything I say, but I always like to leave a little room for magic / divine intervention / the universal energy that flows through us all, so if that's something you're into, there's space for you here, too, because no matter what belief system you've cultivated in your life, I think we can all agree that writing can be difficult sometimes, some might even say painful. I intend to convince you that you don't have to suffer.

The first step toward freedom from suffering is to train your mind to see clearly (to recognize what's real, to notice your mental habits, and to gently disentangle from the stories that keep you stuck). In Buddhist teachings this is referred to as *Right View*, the wisdom to perceive reality without the distortions of your expectations, fears, or conditioning. (This is an idea we will circle back to throughout the book.) Training in Right View begins with the regular practice of mindfulness meditation.

Mindfulness meditation provides a refuge from the modern onslaught of attention-grabbing media streams, news cycles, and alerts, but anyone who's ever tried to meditate routinely knows that's easier said than done. We'll talk about how to get consistent with both writing and meditation in the coming chapters, but for right now I want to share with you the difference that regular meditation has made in my writing and my life.

## MEDITATION CHANGED MY LIFE

It took me a long time to establish a regular meditation routine. After attending my first daylong mindfulness retreat in 2005, I set an intention to meditate every day, which quickly devolved into once a week, which eventually became "sometimes," which in truth meant rarely. I knew meditation was good for me, and I felt the positive effects when I did it, but for about a decade I just couldn't seem to make a habit of it. Life was busy.

By 2016 I was working full-time, had two adorable kids, and was deep into the novel that would become my debut, but I was struggling. The short stories I wrote were rejected time and time again. I was getting up early to write before work because it was the only time I could consistently carve out. Six mornings a week I would drink a cup of coffee while I wrote in my journal, and as soon as the caffeine kicked in, I would close the journal, open up my laptop, and get writing. That year, as an experiment, I decided to wedge ten minutes of meditation into my routine after I finished journaling and before I opened my laptop. Just ten minutes.

As I embraced this practice, my writing (and my life) shifted. The changes were small at first but compounded over time. I figured out my novel, finished it, and found an agent. A piece of flash fiction I wrote was not only published, it was nominated for a Pushcart Prize. I wrote a second, far more complex novel in a fraction of the time it took me to write the first. That first novel, *142 Ostriches*, won the WILLA Award for Women Writing the West. My blog was listed by *Writer's Digest* as one of the 101 Best Websites for Writers. I began teaching at conferences and online summits. I started a coaching business so I could help other aspiring authors finish their novels, and have since worked with so many amazing writers.

When I looked back at what had changed, what had finally clicked into place to bring all these wonderful developments about, I didn't immediately see a connection to my meditation practice. Correlation is not causation, but when I really thought about the specific ways that my writing had improved, I saw over and over the subtle influence of mindfulness and how it had helped me to:

- drop into a deep state of focus and get my first drafts done so much faster;
- get comfortable with discomfort so I could write scenes with more compelling conflict;
- recognize all the things I used to think were "writer's block," set them aside, and keep writing;
- understand my emotions and stay with them long enough to find words to describe them effectively, which made my characters much more dynamic and interesting;
- read over my drafts with a more discerning eye so that I do FAR fewer rounds of revisions; and
- deal with the fact that writing can be hard and rejections are part of the job description.

Once I realized the specific ways that mindfulness had helped me as a writer, I wanted to share the practice with the writers I was coaching. But it's one thing to experience something and quite another to teach it, so I enrolled in a two-year mindfulness meditation teacher certification program at the Greater Good Science Center at UC Berkeley, where I studied with Jack Kornfield and his partner Tara Brach. I began bringing meditation to the forefront of how I worked with clients and saw amazing results, over and over again.

Even though most of the clients I work with have little to no experience with mindfulness when they first find me, they quickly experience the benefits of adding meditation to their writing routine. In some ways, having no experience makes things easier because you can more readily tap into the mental openness that comes when you decide to explore something new.

In the beginner's mind there are many possibilities, but in the expert's there are few.
—ZEN MASTER SHUNRYU SUZUKI

If that's not you, if you already have a solid meditation practice under your belt, there's plenty here for you, too. Unlike other kinds of coaches, I have no reason to "break" people of habits learned from other mentors or teachers. Instead, you will build on your practice, bringing more awareness to how the meditation you're already doing can help you write more and suffer less. The more you can come to it with an open mind, the more you will take away from this book.

# INTRODUCTION

## ELEMENTS OF MINDFULNESS

Have you brought your beginner's mind? Great. Let's get started.

### HOW TO READ THIS BOOK

There's a story in the Buddhist tradition of a man named Bahiya, who approaches the Buddha to ask how he, too, can become enlightened. The Buddha puts him off three times, giving the kinds of answers one might expect from a wise man (advising Bahiya to look within, to train himself to be mindful). But Bahiya is insistent. He basically says: *Look, we could both die at any moment, so let's cut to the chase.* To which the Buddha replies that enlightenment is about stripping away all the mental clutter and getting down to what is true in each moment. "Just this," he says. Satisfied, Bahiya thanks him and is then promptly killed by a cow.

I like this story not just because of the way it ends (I mean, Bahiya's instincts about his impending doom were eerily prescient), but also because it speaks to a truth about mindfulness that is important to keep in mind: just this. It's another way of presenting the idea of Right View, of seeing things as they truly are, in the present moment.

Just this moment. Just this breath.

When we're writing, it's just this sentence, just this one idea.

The hard part (and the reason it's entirely possible to spend your whole life practicing meditation and/or writing and still feel like a novice sometimes) is that every moment is new, every moment requires that we give it our attention without getting sucked into thoughts about the past or worries about the future.

You could say that "just this" is the guiding principle of this whole book: get focused, turn that attention to what's happening in this moment, and choose wisely how to respond. Every meditation in this book, every writing exercise comes back to "just this." Each chapter will take you deeper into the ways that mindfulness can help you write more and suffer less by presenting a type of meditation for you to try in support of your craft, all of it basically coming down to "just this."

At the end of each chapter, I will share some exercises you can use to implement and play around with the ideas I've presented. You might even call them assignments. Try the ones that appeal to you; then maybe try the ones that don't. I've included some space in the book to jot down ideas and reflections, but you might also consider procuring a notebook to give yourself more room to play with thoughts as they arise. Above all, this book is an invitation to try new things, to have fun and get curious.

Each of the six chapters builds on what came before, so

it makes sense to work through the book sequentially. It also makes sense to give yourself time between chapters to practice what you've learned. How much time is up to you. You could take a day, or a week, or a month, but no matter how quickly or slowly you decide to move through the material, it would almost certainly be beneficial for you to circle back and revisit sections in the future. You will be a different person in a year, a different writer. Thus the lessons you take away from subsequent readings will be different.

To help you revisit the lessons of this book with ease, I've included an appendix with succinct versions of the core meditation practices of each chapter. I strongly suggest you read through the entire book first (the meditations will be more powerful if you understand the context), but if you're feeling impatient, or like maybe death is coming for you, I suppose you could jump right to the back, little Bahiya. Just take care if you find yourself in close proximity to a cow.

## KNOWING THE MIND THAT WRITES

In order to write more and suffer less, you need a basic understanding of how your brain operates: what it wants, what it fears, what it's really up to when you sit down to write, because whether you're aware of it or not, your thoughts, moods, and attention patterns shape everything you put on the page.

This book isn't about fixing your mind or making it conform to some imagined criteria. The very idea is anathema to my personal belief that you are enough, exactly as you are. Instead, this book is an invitation to get curious. Mindfulness gives you the ability to observe your inner world with a little more kindness and clarity. Once you can see what's happening in your mind, without judgment (once you get down to "just this"), you can start to make intentional choices about how you write and how you relate to your work, which in turn will lead to all kinds of practical on-the-page benefits.

Let's begin by getting to know the mind that writes.

It's important to recognize that much of the evolution of the human brain took place in prehistory. More than forty thousand years ago, small clans of early humans gathered around crackling fires. Some painted symbols on cave walls: animals, handprints, swirling shapes. Others told stories about the sun and moon. Long before the written word, humans used creativity and storytelling to solve problems, make sense of their experiences, and forge connections. This creative instinct, our drive to express, share understanding, and connect, is fundamental. If you write, you've felt this: the spark of a new idea or image, the urge to speak something true and unique about the world.

But alongside this creative spark often come questions: Will people like this? Am I talented? Creativity doesn't exist in isolation; humans also crave recognition, connection, and security. Even back in those cave-dwelling days, storytelling wasn't just a personal expression; it must have earned admiration within the community. Approval feels good, and there's nothing wrong with wanting it. But creating for meaning and creating for praise are distinct motivations, often tangled together and difficult to distinguish.

Your mind obscures its own processes, making it tricky for you to notice when your sincere creative impulses shift toward yearning or anxiety. One moment you're flowing with ideas; the next, you're second-guessing yourself. Nothing obvious has changed, but on a deep subconscious level your mind perceives or imagines something as a potential threat and subtly takes control in an effort to protect you, whether the danger is real or not. All this happens without your awareness. One minute you're writing. The next, you're worrying.

This slipperiness of mind is part of being human. Buddhists famously call this restless, noisy mental activity the *monkey mind*, as it swings between thoughts, worries, and desires as if they're tree branches in a forest.

## THE MONKEY MIND

The mind's natural tendency to jump fretfully from past regrets to future worries is nothing new. Even before social media algorithms and the twenty-four-hour news cycle, the human brain was wired to ruminate, imagine, and predict. Modern neuroscientists can observe this mental meandering with functional magnetic resonance imaging (fMRI) and have named the regions of the brain that are involved in wandering reflections the default mode network (DMN), a new description for a long-standing lived experience of what your brain does when you're not focused on a specific task: You daydream, relive memories, and spin scenarios. These are the things that must be stripped away to get down to "just this," to understand the truth of any given moment.

Another fact about the human mind is that it's wired to see the negative in everything. This has served humans well evolutionarily because, for basic survival, it's better to assume that something banal is dangerous than the other way around. As a result, the mind's constant storytelling often tilts toward threat assessment and problem-finding, crafting narratives that aren't always accurate or helpful.

For writers, an untrained monkey mind that's always looking for threats manifests as subtle mental suffering—namely, fear, craving, doubt, and aversion. The mind wanders, replaying criticisms or anxiously projecting future outcomes, trying to resolve the unresolvable. Creativity itself remains vibrant, but becomes obscured by mental chatter. This is perfectly normal, but when you get stuck in a dark frame of mind, writing can feel more like an exercise in self-recrimination rather than joyful, creative exploration. It doesn't have to be this way.

## REDUCING THE NOISE TO BOOST THE SIGNAL

Mindfulness meditation provides practical training to quiet the monkey mind and practice Right View, to see things as they really are, to discern your genuine creative impulses from the distractions fueled by subconscious ulterior motives. Observing your mind with kindness and curiosity, you can learn to gently redirect attention from unhelpful chatter back to the present.

Let's take a moment to dissect the term *mindfulness meditation*.

To be mindful is simply to intentionally be aware of the present moment, without judgment. You can be mindful anytime, whether you're washing dishes, writing a novel, or walking the dog.

Meditation is the act of intentionally setting aside time to practice and cultivate mindfulness. That's it.

Of course, talking about mindfulness meditation is all well and good, but it's important to try it for yourself. So, let's do a simple mindfulness exercise right now.

Wherever you're sitting reading this book, take a few moments to give mindfulness meditation a try. (Here I feel compelled to note the complete impossibility of trying to meditate WHILE reading instructions on how to meditate. To download some free guided Insight Meditations I've created just for readers of this book, visit SitWriteHere.com.)

Here's what to do:

1. Sit comfortably, relaxed but alert.
2. Set a timer on your phone for three minutes.

3. Close your eyes if that's comfortable for you, or just cast your gaze downward to minimize distraction.
4. Take a few slow, deep breaths, then let your breath settle into its natural rhythm.
5. Focus gently on your breathing, noticing sensations at the nostrils, the rise and fall of the chest or belly.
6. When your mind wanders (and it will), gently and kindly redirect it back to your breath.
7. Continue until your timer goes off, gently returning to the breath each time you notice a distraction.
8. Finish by opening your eyes and acknowledging how you feel.

Congratulations! You've just practiced mindfulness meditation. You will spend a lot more time with this practice throughout the book, building on it and exploring different types of meditation, but for right now just check in. What did you notice?

Perhaps your mind was busy, or maybe it settled more easily than you expected. Both experiences, and everything in between, are perfectly normal. Notice how you feel now compared to before you started. Do you feel a bit calmer, more centered, or perhaps simply more aware of your mental state? Even subtle shifts matter.

If the practice felt challenging, know that it does get easier with time. Like learning any new skill, mindfulness requires patience and gentle persistence. Each session is an opportunity to learn about your mind's patterns and gently redirect them toward presence and clarity.

Try this short practice again, either now or at another

convenient moment. Notice how the experience is the same and how it's different. Each mindful breath is a step toward greater awareness, and each step yields benefits, not just in the practice of meditation but in all areas of life, including your writing. Mindfulness isn't something you perfect; it's something you continuously practice. Now we're ready to explore how you can bring this experience and practice into your writing.

## SEEING CLEARLY

As I've already touched on, mindfulness at its heart is about learning to see things as they truly are, in the present moment, without judgment. As the ill-fated Bahiya learned just before his death, it's about getting down to "just this." It sounds simple enough, but in practice, it's quite difficult to see anything as it is because everything you encounter is colored by your past experiences and present conditions. You will explore this concept in greater depth later in the book, but for right now, consider that:

- When you see yourself more clearly, you understand how your own thoughts, emotions, and aversions can influence your writing.
- When you see your characters more clearly, you can appreciate their full complexity.
- When you train to see your work clearly, you can better evaluate what's on the page and what isn't.
- When you come to see your relationship to your work with clarity, you don't confuse your writing with your worth as an individual.

In all these ways, mindfulness enables you to better understand yourself, your characters, your work, and your relationship to your work.

## Seeing Yourself Clearly

The first three chapters of this book are dedicated to the discipline of mindfully seeing within, to understand your own foundations. Writing begins in the mind, which means your habits of mind (your attention, your inner dialogue, your moods) directly affect whether and how you get words on the page. There's a lot to unpack here.

By practicing mindfulness, you become more aware of what's happening inside your head at any given moment. It's difficult to overstate the power of this self-awareness for writers. It helps you to nurture your creativity, to look honestly at the things that sometimes keep you from writing, and to stay with difficult scenes until they're on the page.

Mindfulness also creates a space of choice around your thoughts. Sometimes mindfulness teachers refer to this as "the pause." It's only a fraction of a second, this pause. It's the tiny moment between the stimulus (something happening or a thought arising) and the response (what you do about it). Meditation stretches that pause to more like half a second. That may not sound like much, but half a second (when we consider the speed of neurons) can make all the difference. It gives you a space for choice, allowing you to make a decision on how to act, instead of just reacting mindlessly. In effect, you become more receptive to your creative ideas and less controlled by the negative ones—a huge step toward a healthy writing practice.

## Seeing Your Characters Clearly

Just as mindfulness helps you understand yourself better, it also opens your eyes to the rich inner lives of your characters. In chapter 4 you'll explore how, when you write, you are essentially shining the light of attention on human behavior and emotion.

Here, too, it's all about seeing clearly. Characters come to life when you remember that each one believes they're the hero of their own story, even the antagonists. In other words, every character has their own logic, desires, and justifications. Mindfulness practice can deepen your ability to empathize with these perspectives by training you to suspend judgment and really observe what's driving a person. Instead of labeling a character "good" or "evil" and leaving it at that, you become curious about why they are the way they are. This not only makes your characters more believable and relatable, it can also foster compassion, a reminder that all people, whether fictional or real, have reasons for being who they are. By seeing them clearly, in all their complexity, you do justice to their stories.

## Seeing Your Work Clearly

Once you've drafted your story, poem, or essay, a new challenge arises: Can you see what you've created with clear eyes? Every writer knows how difficult revising and editing can be, in part because you are so close to your own work. You know what you meant to say; you see the rich vision in your mind, but is that what's actually on the page? In chapter 5 we will explore how mindfulness can help you answer that question honestly. It takes training to perceive your writing as it truly is, rather than as you intended it to be. Through practice, however, you can train your mind to see what's really on the page and what isn't. This is the key to efficient and effective revision.

## Seeing Your Relationship to Your Work Clearly

Writing can be an emotional roller coaster. There are moments of elation that can range from finding the perfect word to receiving a favorable review, and moments that test your spirit. Rejections, criticisms, or long periods of creative doubt can be difficult to endure. Mindfulness helps by teaching *equanimity*: a quality of balance and nonattachment. As you will investigate in chapter 6, equanimity means understanding that you are not your work. Your stories, essays, or poems are deeply important, yes, but they do not define your worth. Success or failure on the page is not a verdict on you as a human being. This clarity (separating self from product) allows you to ride the emotional waves of the writing life instead of drowning in them.

Mindfulness illuminates that your job is to write with as much joy and ease as possible, not to grasp for validation or run from discomfort. When you really absorb this, you discover a quiet, enduring strength. You write more, and you suffer less. You find the courage to tell the stories you need to tell. You submit your work and start new projects, understanding that each piece is just one expression of an ever-growing talent. You face critiques with curiosity and gratitude for the perspective they offer. You celebrate wins with humility and perspective.

There's so much that mindfulness can do for you as a writer, but there are also misconceptions about what the practice is (and isn't). I'd like to take a moment here to clarify a few of the terms used throughout the book and to dispel some common fallacies about meditation.

## MISCONCEPTIONS ABOUT MEDITATION

When I was in college, in the mid-1990s, I caught a ride from Portland to San Francisco with some friends of friends. One of them was a "trustafarian" stoner kid who called himself (loudly and often) a Buddhist. When we stopped to pee, he wandered off into the woods and came back twenty minutes later, eyes bloodshot, without his shoes. I asked him if he wanted help finding them. He just smiled, pressed his palms together, and bowed, insisting he would be fine. Everything was peace and love and I really shouldn't worry so much about earthly possessions. Ugh.

All I could think was how, sooner or later, the dude was going to need something on his feet, and the only kind of person who wouldn't worry about lost shoes was someone who could easily (even though they had no job to speak of) just buy another pair. For a long time, this was the image I held in my head whenever I heard someone talk about mindfulness: privileged, spoiled, wasteful.

More than anything, that perspective was born of my own ignorance, and I regret that my dismissal of mindfulness as something reserved for entitled potheads kept me from learning more for almost a decade. Thankfully, curiosity won out, and in 2005, at a daylong beginner's course, I was introduced to the version of mindfulness I would go on to study intensively.

There are many different kinds of meditation, and you should do whatever is right for you, even if that means wandering off into the woods and coming back without your shoes. But since I've set myself the task of drafting an entire book on mindfulness meditation and writing, it seems important to define my terms.

The kind of meditation I practice and teach is called Insight Meditation or sometimes Vipassana Meditation, rooted in the Thai Forest Tradition, which emphasizes awareness of body and mind. You practice by simply sitting still and noticing what's true for you in any given moment. You'll explore this much more in the coming chapters, but in a nutshell, that's it.

What you don't need to practice mindfulness:

- Fancy apps or technology. People have been practicing meditation for thousands of years, long before tech existed. You don't need it. That said, I use a simple meditation timer app on my phone and find it very helpful.

Figure out what works for you, but don't let yourself get too caught up with gadgets.

* Perfect lotus position with your legs folded up like a pretzel. I mean, if you can, and it's comfortable, go for it, but you can feel free to meditate in any position that works for you.

* Bells, mantras, chants, candles, crystals, special scarves, marijuana, expensive teas, or really anything else. I love bells, and have been known to join in a chant from time to time, but you don't need them to meditate. You're just going to sit quietly for a few minutes and try to become more aware of your thoughts. Everything else is gravy.

## Emptying Your Mind

Hopefully you've noticed that I haven't said anything about emptying your mind. A common misconception about mindfulness meditation is that you have to be able to rid your mind of all thoughts. That's a fool's errand, especially if sustained attention is biologically challenging for you. Instead, you're going to practice becoming more aware of where your mind tends to run off to. That simple act of consciously increasing awareness opens up a world of possibilities. If you struggle with attention deficit, the practices in this book can help.

Regular mindfulness practice strengthens the areas of the brain involved in attention and emotional regulation, calming reactive stress centers.[*] It provides a stable anchor, often the breath, to which you can repeatedly return your attention if it

---

* Check out the work of Jon Kabat-Zinn, Sara Lazar, Yi-Yuan Tang, Britta K. Hölzel, and Gaëlle Desbordes for more on this topic.

wanders. Over time, mindfulness fosters clarity, reduces unnecessary suffering, and creates mental space for authentic creative expression. If you keep it up, regular meditation can also lead you into explorations of interconnectedness, gratitude, nonduality, metacognition, gratitude, and compassion (to name just a few). In the traditional Buddhist context, mindfulness is practiced to liberate all beings from suffering, and I strongly urge you to investigate the teachings if you feel called to do so, but for the purposes of this book, we'll be focused on the ways that mindfulness can help us to write more and suffer less.

## "MINDFUL WRITING" IN THERAPEUTIC SETTINGS

As a final note, I'd like to call out that what you'll be practicing here is different from what is traditionally known as Mindful Writing. The term has been around for a while now to describe a therapeutic technique of freewriting to integrate difficult memories and process trauma. There's plenty of research to back up the efficacy of this practice.* Writing about your memories requires you to engage both sides of your brain and can be an excellent tool for regulating yourself when you're dealing with difficult things. I'm all for it, but it's not what I teach.

Now, without further ado, let's jump into the first way mindfulness meditation can help you write more and suffer less. It's time to talk about finding your creative flow.

---

* For more on this, see Karen A. Baikie and Kay Wilhelm, "Emotional and Physical Health Benefits of Expressive Writing," *Advances in Psychiatric Treatment* 11, no. 5 (September 2005): 338–46, and Bridget Murray, "Writing to Heal," *Monitor on Psychology* 33, no. 6 (June 2002): 54.

# CREATIVE FLOW

Let's be real for a second here. If you're going to make progress with your writing, you can't sit around waiting for the perfect moment or hoping for inspiration to strike. You've got to *make* time for your work (on purpose) and then do your best to use that time well. So that's where we're going to start our journey together.

In this chapter, we'll talk about how to carve out writing time in a way that's doable. Then we'll explore how you can incorporate meditation into your routine to nurture a state of flow, so that when you *do* sit down to write, the words actually come.

The meditation I'm going to describe in this chapter is elegant, simple, and straightforward. When you couple it with your writing practice, it becomes a powerful game changer, but your own experience of it will be unique. Questions tend to come up. That's to be expected. Instead of trying to explain everything all at once, I've added a section at the end of this chapter called "You Might Notice . . ." where I'll discuss some of the most common experiences that new meditators and early-stage writers have when they embark on this journey.

Ready? Let's get writing.

## MAKING TIME TO WRITE

To be a writer, you must make time to write on a regular basis, which is different from trying to find time to write. When you "try to find" time to write, what you're actually doing is putting your writing at the bottom of your to-do list, and let's be honest, no one ever gets to the end of their to-do list. You have to *make* time to write. You have to block out the time on your calendar and then guard it like a momma pit bull.

The first step in making time to write is to become more aware of how you're currently filling your days. We're going to talk a lot about awareness of thought (also known as mindfulness) in the coming pages, but to just dip your toe in, start by bringing some awareness to how you are spending your time now.

For some of you, making time to write will involve taking an honest look at how much of your life you spend online. You can think of this as a kind of Right View, of seeing things as they really are and being honest with yourself. Open the screen time tracker on your phone, look at how many hours you spend on social media, cut it in half, and put that amount of time on your calendar with the designation "writing time." For example, if you spend two hours a day scrolling, put a one-hour block of time on your schedule to write.

This will be harder than you think. The people who design the apps on your phone are paid very well to make sure you don't put your phone down. Even if you decide, honestly and with the best of intentions, to only spend one hour on your phone instead of two, you are very likely to lose track of time, or keep saying "just one more minute," until you've mindlessly scrolled right through the hour you had set aside to write.

Social media is the antithesis of mindfulness. Instead of making space for ideas and training yourself to observe thoughts when they arise, social media is designed to keep you endlessly engaged while hardly even noticing what's in front of your face. It pulls you into the comparison game and keeps you dancing like a frantic poodle in search of little heart emojis, all of which just leads to depression and burnout.

Take a moment, right now, to honestly answer these questions for yourself:

How much time (on average) do you spend each week on social media? ______________

Now consider that the average writer, working on a first draft, can write about 500 words an hour, and do the math: [hours a week spent on social media] × 500 = ______________ words per week.

The average novel is about 80,000 words, so the calculation becomes: 80,000 ÷ [words per week] = ______________ (number of weeks to finish a first draft of a novel).

Of course, the calculation will be different if you're working on a screenplay or a collection of poems, but hopefully you can see the larger point here that when you get serious about making time to write, you can see some serious progress pretty quickly.

One of the best things you can do for yourself as a writer is to limit the time you spend on social media. If you can't step away completely, set a timer or delete social media apps off your phone so you can only check them at your desk. Or maybe you commit to not picking up your phone until you've done your writing for the day. You should definitely resist the urge to take your phone to bed. Consider reading before bed. Like, a book. It will feed your creativity instead of draining it, and you'll sleep better. Win-win.

Even if you have your device use under control, it's likely there are other demands on your time. Many of you have external pressures like caring for children or aging parents. You have full-time jobs. You have friends, lovers, or demanding pets. If you can't carve out an extra hour by cutting your scroll time, you may have to make a trade-off. Maybe you take a step back from a hobby or sport. Maybe you find a private place to write on your lunch hour at work. When I was first getting started writing, I decided to give up an hour of sleep.

> ## Nothing will work unless you do.
> —MAYA ANGELOU

For years I got up early to write before the kids woke up. I would put as many words as I could on the page until the first pitter-patter came down the hall, then I switched to making breakfasts, packing lunches, doing the commute to work and back. I didn't sleep enough in those years, but I was determined to make time for my writing, and you can, too. Was it easy? No. Am I glad I pushed through? Absolutely. We'll talk more about how to show up for your writing time in chapter 3, but first, it's worth taking a moment to talk more generally about routines.

Routines can be tremendously useful. In the same way that brushing your teeth, washing your face, and putting on pajamas at roughly the same time every night clues your brain in to the fact that it's bedtime, so can your writing routines clue your brain in to the fact that it's time to write. For me, I come into my office with a cup of hot coffee, pull out my journal, and write until one page is filled. Then I sit on my meditation cushion and meditate. When I'm done, I come back to my desk and write for however long I have to write. All these are part of my routine, but the whole sequence of events is triggered by the act of stepping into my office.

Thinking about where you're going to write is equally as important as deciding when. It's helpful to have a designated place. It doesn't have to be fancy, but ideally the room has a door that can be closed. Once you've found a writing space, it's worth taking some time to make it yours. When you grab any old corner of a cluttered guest room or grungy garage, you're sending strong signals to yourself that this thing you're doing, this writing, isn't really important. Even if you're just writing at the kitchen table (which I did for years), take a minute to clean the table before you sit down, make yourself a cup of coffee or tea, and bring a cozy blanket. Make it your space, if only for the duration of your writing time.

The downside to routines is how easily they can be disrupted. Life happens. Whenever you get derailed from your writing routine, be kind with yourself. No routine exists in perpetuity. All things are impermanent. Just keep coming back to the work; tweak and modify your routine as needed to find what works now, today. Try not to cling to what worked last month.

There's a story I love about a Buddhist monastery where the community had taken in a stray cat that was much adored, but the cat had a habit of wandering around the temple during meditation sessions, pressing its little body against the monks and crawling over laps. It was very distracting and so the community decided that when the bell was rung for meditation, someone would be in charge of leashing the cat, so it would settle in one place and not be disruptive. The routine became: ring the bell, leash the cat, meditate. Then one day, they couldn't find the cat. They rang the bell, but felt they couldn't meditate until the cat had been found and leashed. They had lost sight of why they started leashing the cat in the first place.

Sometimes routines have to change to stay useful, so embrace them, use them, but don't get so caught up in them that you forget why you set them up in the first place. Instead of running on autopilot, mindfulness invites you to check in: *Is this routine still serving me?*

Pause here and consider what routines you have around writing. Do you have a designated time? A designated place? If not, what might your writing routine look like? What would it take to make it happen?

———————————————————

———————————————————

———————————————————

———————————————————

———————————————————

It's worth mentioning, too, that you don't have to write every day, no matter what Stephen King says. I can't tell you how much it breaks my heart to see a writer trying to juggle their creative dreams along with family, work, and God knows what else, and then discount themselves as a writer because they "only" write four days a week.

The most important thing when trying to make progress on a writing project is consistency. Ideally you could write several times a week, but if it's once a week, or even once a month, you are still a writer. The problem with writing less frequently is that when you do sit down to write, there's a whole ramping-up process that needs to happen. You have to remember what you were working on, go back and read pages. It's a lot of work and eats up valuable writing time. For most people, writing twice a week is enough to avoid that ramping-up process, but you will need to experiment to find what works for you, then stick with it.

## FIND YOUR FLOW

Now that you've gotten serious about carving out some time to write, let's make that time as productive as possible by teaching you to tap into a state of creative flow.

If you've been writing for any length of time, you may have already experienced flow, where words come easily, ideas float up out of nowhere, and time seems to disappear. Most writers are familiar with this phenomenon, but they don't expect it every time they sit down to write. When it happens, it feels like magic, as if the stars aligned or the muses saw fit to smile down upon you. I am truly, deeply excited to tell you that tapping into that state of flow is something you can train yourself to do. Not once in a while, not when the conditions are right, but every damn time you sit down to write, because it's not magic, it's focus.

The word *flow* was first used as a psychological term by the Hungarian American psychologist Mihaly Csikszentmihalyi, who heard the word over and over from people describing the mental state of being fully immersed in an activity, of existing in that sweet spot where challenge and skill are perfectly balanced and everything just seems to unfold with ease.* What he found as his research progressed was that flow is directly related to focus, and that our capacity for focus is limited.

In later work, Jeanne Nakamura and Csikszentmihalyi estimated that the human brain can only process information at a rate of about 120 bits per second.† That's a million times slower than your average 2025 laptop. What's more, our limited human bandwidth gets used up pretty quickly. Just listening to another person talk requires an estimated 60 bits per second.

But here's the exciting part: When your working memory is fully engaged in a challenging but manageable task (some-

---

* Mihalyi Csikszentmihalyi's *Flow: The Psychology of Optimal Experience* was first published in 1990.
† Jeanne Nakamura and Mihalyi Csikszentmihalyi, "The Concept of Flow," in *Handbook of Positive Psychology*, eds. C. R. Snyder and Shane J. Lopez (Oxford University Press, 2002), 89–105.

thing like writing), the activity in the prefrontal cortex, the area of the brain responsible for self-reflection and time perception, temporarily decreases. This short-term reduction in location-specific brain activity is called *transient hypofrontality*.

In short, when you're in a deeply focused state, there's just not enough processing power in your brain to sustain the yapping of your inner critic or to keep track of trivial things like time. Your lived experience of this is that you're more open to creative ideas and hours can go by in what feels like a few minutes. Flow is a super-creative, highly productive state of being.

> [Meditation] helps train the mind to settle and focus and be more perceptive, more aware, which is of course very helpful for the writing process.
> —RUTH OZEKI

When you practice mindfulness meditation regularly, you are nurturing a deep state of focus that is the very foundation of flow. This heightened attention gives you agency over your own mind. It gives you the ability to see "just this" and to choose, over and over, to release distractions and immerse yourself deeper and deeper into your writing. Let's put it into practice.

## INTRODUCTION TO INSIGHT MEDITATION

If you took the time to do the three-minute meditation in the introduction, this will be familiar. It's basically the same practice, but for a longer period of time and with a few options for you to experiment with in terms of where you rest your attention.

The invitation is to try it right now, but if that's not possible, decide when you will set aside five to fifteen minutes to give it a try, maybe even put it on your calendar (and don't forget you can check out the free guided meditations I've created for you at SitWriteHere.com).

Here's what you do:

1. Set your timer. If you're new to meditation, start with five minutes. If you have some meditation experience already, try fifteen minutes.

2. Find a comfortable place to sit. If you're in a chair, plant both feet on the floor. Rest your hands in your lap. Close your eyes if that's comfortable, or just cast your gaze downward to minimize distraction.

3. Choose something to rest your attention on. This will be your anchor, your home base, the place to bring your mind back when it wanders (because it will). When I introduced this practice earlier, I suggested that you focus on your breath because noticing the sensations of breathing is a great way to anchor your practice, but if you find that it makes you uncomfortable, there's nothing wrong with you. When I first started meditating, focusing on my breath made my chest feel suddenly and uncomfortably constricted. With time (we're talking years) that sensation faded, but for a long while I focused my attention on the sounds in the room, waiting patiently for each sound to rise and pass away. Some of my students like to use a mental countdown, starting at

ten and working their way down to zero, then starting again at ten. You can also try pairing the count with your breath. Experiment to find what works for you.

4.  Do your best to stay focused on your anchor, knowing that your mind will wander. Like, a lot. This is your monkey mind doing what it does. This is not a sign that you're doing it wrong. In fact, it's quite the opposite. Every time you notice your mind has wandered, THAT is your moment of mindfulness. You have become aware of your own thoughts. Congratulations!

5.  Now you have a choice: Follow that thought down whatever rabbit hole it was taking you, or let it go and come back to your anchor. The invitation for the duration of the meditation is to come back to the anchor, repeatedly, as many times as you need to. Some days will be easy, and you will find that you can stay with your anchor for longer periods. Some days will feel ridiculous, as if you've hardly even settled on your anchor before your thoughts are off and running again. There's a useful energy in that, so don't beat yourself up. Just keep coming back to the anchor.

6.  When the timer goes off, open your eyes and turn your attention to your writing.

**The power of this practice is in the final step.** When you finish your meditation, resist the urge to just shake your head and go about your work as you always do. Instead, as you move directly into your writing, imagine that you're still meditating, but the anchor (your center of focus) is now your work.

As you start typing, thoughts will arise, but in your heightened state of awareness you can notice those thoughts, let them go, and come back to the writing.

What you will very likely notice is that the overwhelming majority of the thoughts that come up will be distractions of one kind or another. This is your brain's totally normal reaction to you doing something challenging. We'll talk about this more in chapter 4, but for now just notice the uncanny coincidence of how, when it's time to write a difficult scene, you suddenly realize you need to go grocery shopping. Then let that thought go and keep writing.

## HOW MUCH MEDITATION IS ENOUGH?

Writers often ask if the five to fifteen minutes of meditation I've suggested here should be in addition to the hour of writing. Ideally, yes. The meditation is preparation time. That said, if you only have an hour, I still suggest doing a ten-minute meditation at the start. You will get much more writing done in the remaining fifty minutes if you take the time to get focused.

In my experience, both personally and with clients, somewhere between five and fifteen minutes is usually enough time to mentally step away from the stress of everyday life and calm the nervous system so that you can shift your attention to a focused activity (like writing) without getting sucked back into distracting ruminations.

I once had a client who insisted that she just didn't have ten minutes in a day to meditate. She was working too much and barely sleeping, so getting up early didn't appeal to her. After talking through the reality of her daily schedule, she insisted that the only quiet time she had was while she waited for the kettle to boil for tea. She decided to make that her meditation time. Instead of trying to do work on her phone or checking social media while she waited for the water to boil, she would place her hands on the counter, close her eyes, and just notice her breath, notice how the counter felt cool against her palms, notice the clicking sounds of the kettle as it heated. Then she would make her tea and get to work.

Experiment a little to find what works for you. As a rule of thumb, more is better, but any amount is a gift to yourself. As you get some experience with meditation, try sitting for longer periods. See how it affects your focus. Notice how you feel afterward. I hear from writers all the time how amazed they are at the focus they find when they practice meditation before writing. The words come easier, new ideas float up out of nowhere, the hours fly by. It really is remarkable. In truth, you could stop reading right here and walk away a more productive writer, but there is so much more to explore.

In the next chapter, we're going to talk about how to embrace the benefits of allowing yourself to get uncomfortable, because powerful writing often requires us to go straight into the places we'd rather avoid. The good news? You don't have to suffer through it. You can learn to be with the hard parts (mindfully, honestly) and come out the other side with work you're proud of.

## You Might Notice . . .

Now that we've covered the basics of how to make time for your writing and to get super-focused, let's take a moment to acknowledge something important: The practice of meditation is simple, but people are not. If you're new to writing, meditation, or both, there are a few things you might notice as you begin to engage in this practice. You can read through this section now, or just dog-ear the page so you can easily come back to it after you've meditated a few times and questions begin to arise.

## If You're New to Meditation

If you're new to meditation, you may start to notice all kinds of thoughts that you were previously unaware of. It can be disconcerting, especially as the thoughts pertain to your writing.

You may notice doubt or the voice of your inner critic piping up. We're going to talk about those thoughts and more later in the book, but it's important that you know, right from the start, how very normal these thoughts are.

Another thing to keep in mind is that these thoughts only have as much influence as you give them. In the past, it's likely you've subconsciously given them a lot of credence, but as you become more aware of them, that can change.

Here are some of the thoughts writers often notice as they begin writing in a mindful state.

The writing-is-hard-it-would-be-easier-to-do-something-else thoughts:

* *I should check my email, there might be something important.*
* *I should really go fold the laundry.*
* *The kids have been watching TV for so long, I should go play with them.*
* *I need to research [some random fact] before I can keep writing.*
* *I've been meaning to organize the garage.*

These thoughts are sneaky because they're probably true, or at least they feel true in the moment, when your brain is looking for any excuse to do something that feels less daunting than writing. Remember, when these thoughts come up, your brain is trying to make things easier on you. It's a perfectly natural response to a challenging situation. Prepare for it by having a set amount of time in which you plan to write (again, I suggest an hour). Then, when you notice the thoughts, you can acknowledge them and ask yourself, "Can it wait an hour?" Odds are, it can. Let those thoughts go and keep writing. Give yourself that single hour to write and amaze yourself with what you can get done.

The everything-I-write-is-crap-why-am-I-even-doing-this thoughts:

* *That was a terrible sentence I just wrote.*
* *Am I really going to open this story/chapter/poem with that idea?*
* *This is so cliché.*

> • *I'm pretty sure I'm the worst writer ever to try to write any-thing.*

Please know that these thoughts are perfectly normal. They're a sign that you care about the work. The good news? As you practice noticing them and letting them go, you get better at noticing them and letting them go. In time, you'll be able to easily discern them and laugh a little as you recognize how very mundane and common they are.

Remember the story of me crying over the onions? If I had let myself get caught up in the narrative of suffering, I could have easily ushered myself down a mental dark alley, telling myself, *Yes, I know people cry over onions, but this is particularly bad. No one has ever had THIS MUCH trouble or cried SO PROFUSELY while trying to dice onions. There's something wrong with me.* Nonsense, right? Doubt is just a normal human response to hard things. Notice it, know that you are not alone in experiencing it, and keep writing.

All these thoughts (and more) have a sneaky way of presenting themselves as uniquely important. Each one feels like it absolutely must have your attention the moment it arises, so it's easy to get caught up in them. To give yourself a little perspective, you can try categorizing your thoughts. When an idea arises during your meditation, just take a mental step back and consider what type of thought it is.

As an example, imagine you're meditating and you realize you're planning dinner. First of all—congratulations! You noticed that your mind wandered. That is exactly what you're trying to do here: become more aware of your own thoughts. Good work. Now, take a moment to acknowledge the type of thought that carried you away, in this case planning. You might reflect to yourself, *There's my planning mind again*, then let that thought go and come back to your anchor.

When you generalize the thought, it suddenly feels less powerful. It becomes easier to watch it rise and pass away like everything else in this world.

Other categories of thought might include worry, memory, judgment, sensory observation (you notice an itch or hear a dog bark), boredom, doubt, or restlessness. Over time, as you become more aware of your thoughts, categorize them, and let them go, you will start to notice themes. My teacher, Jack Kornfield, calls these your greatest hits. They're the thoughts, or types of thoughts, that play over and over again in your mind.

Categorizing thoughts can help you avoid getting caught up in specific narratives. For example, if in your meditation you realize you're thinking about a friend who's going through a difficult divorce and you're fuming over the details of the relationship's demise, you can pause, notice you're worrying, and recognize that these thoughts are a perfectly normal extension of your love and concern for your friend. You can even say the words in your head, *Oh, there's my worrying mind again*. Then let those thoughts go and come back to your anchor.

It's worth noting that you're not dismissing or discounting the reality that you're worried about your friend, but those worries will still be there when you're done meditating. While you're on the cushion you can let them go and refocus on your anchor. Later in the day, when that worry arises again, you can pick up the phone and call your friend. You're just not going to do it while you're focused on meditating or writing.

Remember, it's a practice. There will be easy days and hard days. Sometimes, at the end of my morning meditation, I press my palms together, give a little bow, and think, *Well, I tried*, because, man, was my monkey mind in full swing. But I know that even the effort of trying, of sitting my butt on the cushion and doing my best to keep coming back to my anchor, means I am practicing doing something that is good for me and for my writing. Other days I find that I actually feel super-focused at the end of a meditation. That's lovely, and it can carry over into the work.

Here are a few of the pleasant thoughts you can expect to encounter when you bring the focus of mindfulness to your writing. I call them the I-just-had-a-great-idea-for-my-story thoughts:

- *Oh! I realize now why this character is such a jerk/hero/ anxious mess.*
- *I hadn't considered that plot twist.*
- *The perfect title just came to me.*
- *Aha! I know how to end this thing!*

Being in this heightened state of focus allows creative ideas to float up seemingly out of nowhere. It feels a little like divine intervention when it happens, like some outside source has seen fit to bless you with a good idea. When you notice these thoughts, *don't* just let them go. Being mindful means giving yourself a moment of choice; you can choose in each instance to let an idea go or follow it. If the thought is useful, go with it. This might mean jumping to the chapter, scene, or stanza for which you have the inspiration, or it could mean just jotting down the idea so you can come back to it later. You get to decide.

The challenge after experiencing this kind of inspiration is not to cling to that result. If you go into your meditations expecting brilliant insight each time, you're likely to get discouraged if it doesn't come. Remember that every meditation is a unique and fleeting experience.

Do your best to accept what comes, be kind with yourself, and keep practicing. I promise you it will make a difference in your writing, and in your life.

## If You're New to Writing

If you're new to writing, you might notice that it's hard to get started. We talked earlier in the chapter about some practical ways to make time for your writing. Here are a few more things that can help when you're just getting started:

- Tell people that you're a writer.
- Nurture your creativity.
- Keep a notebook for creative thoughts.
- Follow the enthusiasm.

### Tell People That You're a Writer

If you've never before called yourself a writer, it can feel scary. You might notice some anxiety or trepidation when someone asks what you do and you want to say *writer*, but feel like you can't, so I'm going to let you in on a little secret: If you write, you're a writer. That's it. That's all you have to do.

Of course, in the purest implementation of Buddhist thought, it's folly to identify as a writer, or even as a living being distinct from any other being on Earth, but for the purposes of this book, I'm assuming you're not a monk. You are simply a layperson dedicated to putting words on pages, so go ahead and call yourself a writer. To do so is to honor the fact that writing is something you enjoy doing, whether for yourself or for publication.

So, if you write (at all) and you haven't yet made the jump to telling the people in your life that you're a writer, I would like to propose that this might be a good time.

You will be much more likely to hit your writing goals if you have the support of the people in your life. Go ahead and take that plunge. Change your bio on social media, print up business cards, and the next time someone asks what you do, tell them that you're a writer (even if you're paying the bills as a lawyer/mechanic/bartender). Notice how it feels, notice if you feel compelled to justify, explain, or minimize the fact that you're a writer. If you're not ready to make a grand declaration just yet, that's okay, too. Notice that. Remember how the Buddha said, "Just this." In that moment of discomfort "this" might be some resistance. Simply pay attention to what it feels like in your body. You don't even have to do anything about it, if you don't want to. As you'll learn in the coming chapters, that act of noticing is how we bring the strength and power of mindfulness into our writing lives to deal with everything from impostor syndrome to character development.

When you're ready, start by saying you're "taking some time to write." Notice how that feels. Hopefully you will be met with support, but I can't promise it. If you've never before made space for yourself as a creative person, you might be met with some resistance. External pressures for you to stay who you've always been can be strong.

When you announce to your friends and loved ones that you want to be someone slightly different from who you've always been, they might subconsciously fear how the shift will affect them, how their relationship with you might change. Try to see this as a compliment. They like the you you've always been. It doesn't mean you have to remain unchanged just to spare them a bit of discomfort.

If old friends get weird about your growing commitment to writing, find support in new acquaintances. Join a writing group, online or in person. Say hello to that other writer you always see on Sundays at the coffee shop, and when they ask if you're a writer, too, say yes. Don't qualify it by saying you've never been published, or that you only write on the weekends. Just say yes. Notice how it feels.

The truth is, you will become a different person as you step into being a writer. If it feels right, if it's what you want, nobody has the right to tell you that you can't or shouldn't. You have one short life to live, my friend, and I can tell you from experience that if a story has its hooks in you, you're screwed. Sorry not sorry. It's not going to go away. You might be able to ignore it, but it will always be there, clinging like cigarette smoke to your hair and clothes, until you get it onto the page. You have to write it.

Remember: *If you write, you're a writer.* There is simply nothing else you need to do to claim that title. You don't have to be published (ever). You don't even have to let anyone read your work. All you have to do is write. If you need permission, here it is: You can call yourself a writer. If anyone takes issue with that, or gives you a hard time, you tell them to take it up with me.

## Know That You Are Creative

There comes a time in every writer's life when the urge to create is present without any specific direction. These are the times when it's important to nurture your creativity and strengthen your inner storyteller.

Creativity is not some heavenly gift that you either have or you don't. It's simply the ability to generate new ideas, connections, or solutions. And it's not just about making art. Whether you're inventing a fictional world, negotiating a business deal, or devising a way to get your kid to brush her teeth, creativity helps you to figure things out. If you've ever solved a problem, you are creative. It's a gift we're all born with.

Spend five minutes watching kids horse around and you'll see how ideas roam freely without constraint. Children make up rules as they go, bringing in aliens, officers, and mermaids as needed. We all start off with that ability, but not all of us are encouraged to nurture it. If you grew up in a household where modes of thinking were strictly limited, where fanciful or ridiculous ideas were dismissed, it's possible you didn't get a lot of opportunity to engage in imaginative play. That's okay. The ability to have fun with ideas is still inside you. Creativity can be cultivated.

The best way to build (or rebuild) your creativity is to engage in play. For many adults, this can feel like a nonstarter. If you're out of practice, the idea of unstructured mental frolicking can be unnerving. It's entirely possible that your brain will go into protective mode and tell you that being silly or playful is a waste of time. It might try to tell you that you should be doing something more serious or productive, but once you become mindful of that pattern, you can simply notice it and let it go.

Here are a few games you can try to get your creative juices flowing.

## What's the Story?

Go out to dinner (alone or with a friend who's willing to play along) and pick a couple at a table on the other side of the room (it's important that they not be able to hear you). Name them. Tell their story. Make it as outlandish and ridiculous as you can. "That woman over there? That's Orianna. She designs shoes for Russian oligarchs. **Yes, and** she's in witness protection because . . ." Whatever comes to mind, roll with it.* If you imagine that the guy sitting on the other side of the restaurant is an axe murderer, say, "**Yes, and . . .** the woman sitting next to him is an undercover cop. **Yes, and** her mother was his first victim. **Yes, and . . .**" Keep it going as long as you can.

## The "What If" Game

Ask yourself, "What if?" What if aliens landed on your roof tonight? What if your husband's other spouse knocked on the door during dinner? What if you found an actual treasure map?

## Smooth Jazz and Rhinos

My family and I invented this game during the COVID lockdown. It's best played with a few people, and kids are great at

---

* The phrase "yes, and" is one of the foundational principles of improvisational theater. It's a great way (for actors and writers alike) to stay open, build momentum, and create without fear of taking a wrong turn. When the next line is always "yes, and . . ." there are no wrong turns.

it. One person poses a problem, the more silly/trivial/ridiculous, the better. Examples might be, "My socks won't stay up," or "I can't get rid of the crabgrass in the yard," and then you go around the table, each person proposing a ridiculous solution. For example, "Play smooth jazz to stay relaxed when your socks fall down," or "Bring in some rhinos to eat the crabgrass." For some reason, the solutions my kids proposed always included smooth jazz and rhinos, hence the name of the game.

Give yourself permission to be silly. Use your mindfulness practice to notice if being ridiculous makes you uncomfortable. You might find yourself thinking, *This is stupid*. For some people, resistance shows up as a physical tightness in the chest or belly, or maybe a general sense of anxiety. Notice those thoughts and sensations, and then see if you can let them go. Bring your mind back to the creative play and intentionally relax the muscles in your body. Trust yourself and try to enjoy the process.

Writers are creative not because they've been granted some special gift but because they're mindful of their thoughts (whether they call it mindfulness or not). They've learned to notice and give attention to the wild and crazy ideas that float through their heads.

## Keep a Notebook for Those Creative Thoughts

Everyone has weird thoughts sometimes. You don't have to admit it. You might not even be aware of them, but they're there, and if you haven't trained yourself to notice them and write them down, they just flit through and are quickly replaced by other thoughts.

The best way to build a practice of noticing and honoring your ideas is to always have a notebook and pen with you. I keep one in every room, my car, and my purse. When you have a random thought, or remember a strange dream, jot it down. Start a collection of these notes in a folder and label it "story ideas." You can use your phone to capture ideas, too, using a notes app or by texting yourself ideas, but I strongly suggest that when you get home or back to your desk, you make sure to put the ideas on paper and store them with the rest in your idea file. Try to collect them all in one place.

Every now and then, when you're looking for inspiration, flip through that folder. Here are a few notes I've left for myself over the years:

- a tree that walks across the street in the night
- fire crabs that live in a volcano
- artwork that comes to life

No idea is too ridiculous (or banal) to make it into the file. To be clear, you will never use 99 percent of these ideas. That's not the point. The point is noticing them, and caring enough to write them down so that when that 1 percent idea, the one that will blossom into your next writing project, pops into your head, you notice and write it down. You don't just let it flit through your brain, only to be replaced by your mental to-do list or the lyrics to Beyoncé's "Texas Hold 'Em."

### Follow the Enthusiasm

Once you start noticing all the ideas you have, you'll be faced with a new dilemma. Which one do you actually want to write about? Which idea should you pursue? The answer is always: Follow the enthusiasm.

The word "enthusiasm" comes from the Greek word that

means "to be inspired or possessed by a god," so you can think of enthusiasm as divine direction, a nudge from the Almighty, or the universe, or your subconscious, or whatever source of power you put your faith in.

Much like creativity, enthusiasm can grow quiet in adulthood, so don't worry if you don't immediately feel a passionate call toward any specific idea. Your creative, exuberant self is inside you somewhere, it just takes a little intention and observation to reconnect with it. To tap into your enthusiasm, consider all the ways your life could have gone, all the different choices you've made up to this point. But for a few key decisions, you would have found different careers, different lovers, different lifespans. There's a long list of lives you might have lived.

What paths did you almost take in your life? Or if it's a stretch to say you almost took them, what paths sparked your curiosity as a child? Assuming resources, time, ability, or reality itself weren't in your way, what careers might you have taken up? When you think about those things, notice if you have a reaction (physical, emotional, or mental) to those ideas. This is a simple way to engage self-awareness as a guide.

For me the list looks something like this:

- Archaeological anthropologist (I find the human fossil record fascinating)
- Ecologist in the Amazon (was I the only one obsessed with the 1992 movie *Medicine Man*?)
- Badass outlaw with hideouts in the desert (blame the Westerns I watched with my dad as a kid)
- Landscape designer/groundskeeper at a botanical garden (because plants)

- Librarian (because books)
- Captain of the *USS Enterprise* (I *know* the job is taken, I still wanted it)
- Extreme athlete (I kind of always wanted to be a rock climber or distance swimmer)

When I look at this list, I feel my enthusiasm stir. It feels like a flutter in my chest. When I notice that reaction, I know I'm onto something. There were good reasons I didn't pursue each of these careers, but there's still a part of me that is curious.

That's the spark of enthusiasm. Then ask: "What if?" Follow that up with a "Yes, and . . ." and you've got the start of a story.

- What if an archaeological anthropologist uncovered an alien skeleton? Yes, and it started communicating telepathically . . .
- What if a librarian found a book of spells? Yes, and she used it to become president of the United States . . .

These ideas would clearly need work to become full-fledged stories, but I'm interested in these worlds and eager to play around with them.

As you spend more time as a writer, these skills (calling yourself a writer, nurturing your creativity, capturing ideas, and following the enthusiasm) will become second nature, but to get there you will need to practice. Be gentle with yourself and try to lean into the fun of it all.

## PRACTICE & REFLECT

Take some time before moving ahead to practice what you've learned so far and reflect on how you'd like to integrate meditation into your writing routine.

### MEDITATE AND WRITE

In the next couple of days, block out some time to meditate and write. Start by setting a timer for ten minutes to practice Insight Meditation before you write (and don't forget to check out SitWriteHere.com for some free guided meditations I've created just for the readers of this book).

INSTRUCTIONS:

1. Get comfortable. Sit in a chair with your feet on the floor or on a cushion with your legs crossed. Let your hands rest gently in your lap.
2. Choose an anchor. Focus on your breath, the sounds in the room, or even a mental countdown from ten to zero.

3. Observe without judgment. When your mind wanders (because it will), simply notice the thought, acknowledge it, and gently return to your anchor.

4. When the timer goes off, consider that you're not ending the meditation so much as shifting the anchor. Instead of focusing on your breath, or the sounds in the room, you will focus on your writing. Thoughts will still arise, you're simply going to notice them. If they're useful, follow them, if not, let them go and keep writing.

5. Do this for one hour.

When your hour of writing is up, take a few minutes (five at the most) to reflect on how it went. It can be interesting to write down these reflections so you can refer back to them in the future.

REFLECTION QUESTIONS:

• What did you notice about your thoughts?

____________________________________

____________________________________

____________________________________

____________________________________

____________________________________

____________________________________

• How did it feel to bring your attention back to your anchor?

____________________________________

____________________________________

_______________________

_______________________

_______________________

_______________________

_______________________

- Did you experience frustration, curiosity, or ease?

_______________________

_______________________

_______________________

_______________________

_______________________

_______________________

- How does this practice compare to the way you usually approach writing?

_______________________

_______________________

_______________________

_______________________

_______________________

_______________________

This last question can be useful in helping you to see the ways in which your approach to writing is shifting.

There is no right or wrong way to do this exercise. Just observe and reflect. With time and practice, mindfulness will become a natural part of your writing routine, helping you focus, stay present, and approach your work with greater ease.

## TAKE NOTES

Buy yourself a small notebook (or five). They don't have to be fancy. Simple spiral-bound, pocket-size pads from the grocery store will do. Put one wherever you spend time: by your bed, in the car, in your purse/briefcase/backpack. Always carry a pen or pencil. Start writing down the ideas that come to you, no matter how lame/dull/ridiculous they may seem at the time. It's not about what you write, it's about building the practice of noticing ideas. When a notebook gets full, pull out the pages with ideas (you can trash the old grocery lists and doodles that will inevitably end up in there, too) and put them in a folder titled "Story Ideas."

## PLAY A GAME

Take some time to build your creativity by playing one of the games mentioned in this chapter:

- **What's the Story?**: Make up a story for a stranger (or strangers), the wilder, the better. Keep it going as long as you can with, "Yes, and . . ."
- **The "What If" Game**: Come up with as many "what ifs" as you can throughout your day. Write them down.
- **Smooth Jazz and Rhinos**: For 2+ players. One player poses a problem. The other players come up with the goofiest, most impractical solutions they can think of.

Notice any resistance that comes up when you play, either as admonishing thoughts or as tension in the body. See if you can soften and release that discomfort and allow yourself to enjoy play for the sake of play.

## THE PATH NOT TAKEN

Make a list of lives you might have lived.

______________________________________________

______________________________________________

______________________________________________

______________________________________________

______________________________________________

______________________________________________

______________________________________________

______________________________________________

______________________________________________

______________________________________________

Do any of them still spark excitement? Combine this exercise with the "What If" game and see what stories might be waiting for you.

## TAKE A SOCIAL MEDIA VACATION

See if you can go one week without checking social media. Notice how you feel at the start of the week. Then notice how you feel at the end.

2

# DISCOMFORT AS A PRACTICE

Hopefully you've had a chance to sit with the practices and exercises in the last chapter. From here forward, we're going to build on those practices, so it's important that you take the time you need to gain some comfort with Insight Meditation.

When you're ready, our first step beyond the basics is to get a little uncomfortable, and I totally get it if you're thinking *pass*, but stick with me for a minute here.

As a human being, you're evolutionarily programmed to avoid discomfort. This aversion is a tapestry of caution woven from your earliest experiences. You avoid weather that is too hot or too cold. You default to social circles that allow you to remain in your comfort zones. You learn as a child not to pick fights. You shy away from the sharp edges of heartbreak and the shadowy corners of fear. Your life, in many ways, is an exercise in evasion, avoiding anything unpleasant while seeking the warmth and safety of the familiar.

But as a writer, you don't have the luxury of avoiding trouble, because conflict is the very essence of story. If your narrative is devoid of difficult emotions, writing may seem straightforward, even effortless. But let's face it: A story without conflict is akin to a body without a circulatory system. Conflict propels a narrative forward and makes readers want to turn page after page, and if you want any chance of capturing conflict on the page, you have to train yourself to sit with all of life's difficult emotions.

So how do you do that? By sitting perfectly still, even when it's uncomfortable.

Research suggests that emotional pain activates roughly the same areas of the brain as physical pain. This explains why intense emotional experiences, such as a broken heart, can feel physically painful. As an added bonus, emotional pain (think something like social rejection) can be relived repeatedly with a fresh sense of immediacy that generally isn't present when you recall physical pain.* For example, I can remember that time I broke my arm without feeling the sharp torment of it all over again, but if I think back to a time I had a falling-out with a friend, there might still be tears.

But here's the cool part: Because of the way our brains are wired, you can build your tolerance for emotional discomfort by training yourself to sit with minor physical discomforts. This is a powerful practice for anyone, but for writers it has another layer of utility because it allows you to write into all kinds of situations that might otherwise make you too uncomfortable to experience.

---

* I feel like this is one of those instances where science simply quantified something we all knew was true. In this case, credit goes to a study published in *Psychological Science* by Chen et al. (2008), https://pubmed.ncbi.nlm.nih.gov/18816286/. They found that individuals reported higher levels of pain after reliving a socially painful event compared to a physically painful one.

## SELF-CARE (DON'T SKIP THIS PART)

In just a couple pages I'll share with you an easy way to practice getting comfortable with discomfort, but before I do, it's critical to touch on the idea of self-care. Please don't skip this part. It's important.

Since the early 2000s, there's been a surge in scientific study around meditation, and it turns out that adverse effects are not rare. A 2022 US study showed that more than 10 percent of participants who engaged in regular meditation experienced adverse effects that included anxiety, reexperiencing traumas, and emotional sensitivity.* Childhood adversity was associated with higher risk of adverse effects, but it was not required.

Because there's a one in ten chance you might experience some negative effects, we should talk about it. How should you deal with that if you find yourself feeling anxious or triggered? In a traditional Buddhist setting, the advice is to just keep sitting, to watch the difficult emotions rise and pass away, no matter how unpleasant, but this is easier said than done.

A friend of mine once went on a ten-day meditation retreat at a monastery in India and after just two days he found he couldn't stop crying. Not just crying but sobbing. He told me later that he felt his heart was breaking. He was so overwhelmed with sadness that he simply couldn't stay any longer. The monks advised him to stay, said that leaving in that state

---

* This is something that should be talked about more. To read the study, look up Simon B. Goldberg, Sin U. Lam, Willoughby B. Britton, and Richard J. Davidson, "Prevalence of Meditation-Related Adverse Effects in a Population-Based Sample in the United States," *Psychotherapy Research* 32, no. 3 (2021): 291–305, https://doi.org/10.1080/10503307.2021.1933646.

was like getting up off an operating table and leaving in the middle of open-heart surgery, but he just couldn't bear it.

In traditional Buddhist practice the monastery is a setting designed to support members of the community who are moving through difficult things in their meditations, so the monks' advice to push through made sense in that context, but my friend, being an outsider from New York, didn't understand or trust that support in a way he might have if he had been living at the monastery for a long time before facing this emotional challenge. He felt adrift in a way that was deeply upsetting so, for him, leaving (and reaching out to talk about the experience with friends) was the right thing to do.

> If you have not sobbed,
> you have not yet begun to meditate.
> —AJAHN CHAH

I have another friend in California who, when faced with a similar experience of being overwhelmed during his meditations, set his intention to double down, to fully experience every emotional pain that arose every time he sat down to meditate. This guy was also an athlete and a master at mind over matter, but it was hard on him. He told me he would cry deeply every time he meditated, for years. Years! It's worth noting that he enlisted the help of both a Western therapist and a Buddhist mentor to help him through this, but still it sounded like it was very unpleasant and is not something I would recommend.

I share these stories so that if the practice you're about to learn brings up some big emotions, you will know that it's totally normal. In chapter 4, we'll talk about how tapping into stored emotions can allow you to release them and feel better, but I will just reiterate here that if you do find yourself consistently overwhelmed by emotion every time you meditate, it would probably be a good idea to bring in a professional to go with you on this journey.

It's worth noting, too, that adverse effects don't have to be so dramatic. When you're sitting, it's totally normal for uncomfortable thoughts to arise. It's important to recognize them and do your best to let them go. Learning to be with discomfort is a journey, one that requires courage, patience, and kindness. As you delve into practices aimed at expanding your comfort zone, it's crucial to do so with compassion. The essence of this practice lies not in the extremes but in the subtle art of nudging your boundaries, ever so slightly, to foster growth and resilience over time.

There are very few ways you can do meditation wrong, but venturing too far into discomfort is one of them. Ignoring your inner signals of distress (whether emotional or physical) can lead you into harmful territory and, in a worst-case scenario, cause physical injury or reopen old emotional wounds. If you push yourself beyond a slightly uncomfortable stretch into a zone of pain, you risk traumatizing yourself, which does not serve you in any capacity.

Even in a non-worst-case scenario, pushing too far out of your comfort zone will be unpleasant enough that you will, on a subconscious level, not want to do it again. This will, in turn, create resistance and keep you from wanting to meditate, and that will mean you miss out on all the benefits meditation has to offer for your writing and your life. So please, for the love of Shakespeare, just go slowly.

Listen to what your mind and body tell you during these

explorations of discomfort. It's not about endurance or the ability to withstand pain; it's about cultivating a deep, compassionate awareness of your limits and learning to gently push against them without crossing into harm.

This goes double for self-judgment or recrimination. The last thing you want to do in your meditation is sit there for ten minutes judging yourself. Is your posture correct? Are you breathing too fast? Is your mind wandering too much? These questions are not helpful and stewing in judgment will just leave you feeling crappy. Of course, for a lot of us, judgment is a habit, and a tough one to break.

## A NOTE ON KINDNESS

The easiest way to unwind judgment is through kindness. We'll talk about this in depth in chapter 6, but it's important that we at least touch on it here, because it's a critical component of seeing things clearly. Consider this example: You're meditating, focused on your breath, and then you realize your mind has wandered and you're planning the epic sandwich you're going to have for lunch. In that moment of realization, you have three choices.

1. Follow that thought. Go ahead and envision that ham and provolone.
2. Let that thought go, and come back to your anchor with kindness.
3. Come back to the anchor while telling yourself what an idiot you are because your mind wandered. I mean, can't you do anything right?

I hope you can see how the third option, while easy to slip into, is not the right choice. Remember that you get better at the things you practice. Don't practice being mean to yourself. Nobody needs that. Instead, ask yourself what's really true in this moment. Is it true that you're an idiot because your mind wandered? Or is that simply what minds do?

By bringing in just the smallest bit of kindness you can see that healthy minds *think*. That's just what they do. No need to beat yourself up for it. So let that thought go and come back to the anchor.

"But my mind wanders constantly!" you say. I hear this a lot. Especially if you have the additional challenge of ADHD or similar attention deficits, it can be frustrating to feel like you just can't get your mind to quiet down. It's okay. Remember that it's not the goal to quiet your mind or (as I often hear people say) "clear" your mind. Your goal is simply to notice what your mind is doing. Where is it going? What are you thinking about?

Keep meditating, be kind to yourself, and talk through what comes up.

## LET'S GET UNCOMFORTABLE

Did you skip the previous section on self-care? I understand that you're excited to get to the actual practice, but you need to go back and read it. It's important.

I'll sit right here.*

Done? Good. The practice I teach for getting comfortable with discomfort is an extension of the Insight Meditation you explored in chapter 1. It's sometimes called Stillness practice, or Formal practice. It's a way of stepping a little more deeply into "just this," of noticing when discomfort arises so that we can choose how to respond with intention, instead of just reacting. This practice builds mental strength that, when applied to our writing, enables us to write even the most difficult scenes.

---

* Forgive me, dear reader! I couldn't help myself.

## MEDITATION: STILLNESS PRACTICE

Keep in mind that engaging in Stillness practice is not about enduring pain or extreme torment. Rather, it's about exploring the boundaries of your comfort zone with curiosity and kindness. Go easy.

1.  Begin by finding a comfortable place to sit.
2.  Set a timer for five to fifteen minutes.
3.  Close your eyes if you wish and allow yourself to settle. Take a few deep breaths. Connect with your body, feel its weight and presence. Choose an anchor for your attention, such as your breath, a sensation in your body, or the ambient sounds around you. This anchor will serve as your point of return, a steady base to which you can come back whenever your mind begins to wander. So far this is precisely what you've been practicing already in this book.
4.  Now you add a deliberate practice of stillness. Once you've begun, try to remain as still as possible, resisting the urge to scratch an itch, adjust your posture, or engage in any other movement.* Sounds easy enough, right? It's actually quite challenging.

Maintain the stillness for the duration of the meditation or until the discomfort edges into pain.

---

* Unless you are an advanced meditator, I suggest you don't try to refrain from the involuntary, subtle movements that come with breathing and swallowing. Let your body be comfortable.

When discomfort arises and you feel the need to adjust, first ask yourself, "Do I really need to move, or can I sit with it?" Notice if the uncomfortable sensation changes as you give it your attention, if it shifts or moves to another part of the body. Begin to learn the difference between a nuisance that can be observed and pain that should be alleviated. If you feel you have reached your limit of what you can sit with, by all means, move. Shift your posture or scratch that itch, then come back to stillness and begin again. But hold out as long as you can.

My teacher, Jack Kornfield, tells the story of when he was fairly new to meditating and found himself sitting with a terribly itchy nose. He didn't scratch it, and it just kept getting more and more itchy until he thought he might die if he didn't scratch it. He finally just surrendered to the fact that he was going to be the first person ever to die from an itchy nose, but then, lo and behold, he survived. The itch passed, as do all things.

The human mind tends to get stuck on discomfort, replaying emotionally painful moments, layering suffering into the narrative with each go-around. With a little perspective, you can see that there are two parts to these painful moments: the thing that happened (the source of the discomfort) and the rumination you bring to it (the suffering).

When talking about pain and suffering, Buddhists sometimes use the metaphor of the first and second arrow. You can think of the thing that causes the initial sadness or discomfort as an arrow landing somewhere in your body. This first arrow is the unavoidable pain of life. You get sick. You get your heart broken. A story you wrote gets rejected.

The second arrow is the one you shoot at yourself. It's the mental and emotional reaction to the initial pain. You might catch yourself thinking, *Why can't I do anything right?* or *I'm such an idiot*, or *Who do I think I am trying to be a writer?* The second arrow is the anger, doubt, and shame one tends to bring to already painful situations.

When you practice mindfulness, you become more able to discern between the source of the pain and the suffering you're layering on top. Then you can choose not to shoot that second arrow. You can feel the pain without adding a layer of avoidable suffering.

We'll get to why all this matters for your characters in just a minute, but I want to talk about your own personal discomforts first. As you work through the practices in this book, you will very likely find yourself taking steps that are unfamiliar and uncomfortable. When you notice discomfort, it's easy to throw up your hands and say "Whelp, I tried, I guess this meditation stuff isn't for me."

Instead of quitting, try flipping the narrative. Recognize that you have become aware of being anxious or sleepy or impatient. That is mindfulness in action. If irritation or lethargy makes a ten-minute sit seem unending, ask yourself, "Could I sit still for one more breath? Then another? Then another?" It's okay to be uncomfortable. In fact, everything you're hoping to accomplish with your writing is on the other side of that discomfort.

Now, let's move away from talking about ourselves and explore why the discomfort of conflict is so important to your story.

## WHY CONFLICT MATTERS TO YOUR STORY

Not long ago I had a client, a talented poet turned fiction writer, who was working on a novel about a Black family living in the late 1800s in the American South. The historical and societal context of their story offered fertile ground for conflict, ripe with the potential to delve into themes of injustice, resilience, and transformation. But every time something terrible happened in their story, they would skip right over it, jumping months, even years after the event, and have their characters reflect on what happened with a great deal of emotional distance.

The writer's reluctance to engage directly with the painful, conflict-ridden moments of the narrative highlights a common challenge that many authors face: the fear of immersing both themselves and their readers in discomfort. It's perfectly natural.

This avoidance, however, fundamentally alters the reader's experience. By leaping over periods of strife and summarizing them after the fact, the writer effectively distances the reader from the characters' emotional journeys. Such an approach may intrigue readers for a bit, but ultimately it leaves the story feeling superficial, as readers are denied the opportunity to fully empathize with the characters and to witness their growth firsthand.

For example, imagine that you've been in a car accident on your way to work. When you tell your colleagues about the mishap a few hours later, the story will be rich with details and emotions. You might be enraged at whoever was at fault, or blame the heavy rainfall. It will likely be a long story and will reveal things about you as a person as you explain how you handled both the crash and the aftermath. Now jump forward five years and consider that, with the passage of time, the entire event has lost most (if not all) of its emotional punch. It will likely be summed up with a few words, like, "Some jerk sideswiped me on the freeway."

When you tell a story from a distance it's much harder to convey its full emotional impact, but when you become an expert observer of emotions, when you get comfortable with even the most unpleasant feelings, there's no story you can't write.

Because all stories are, at their core, about emotions and how our characters respond to them. Recognizing that, embracing it, creates opportunity for emotional engagement, just one of three ways conflict can elevate a story. Conflict can also drive plot and build character. Let's look at each of the three elements in turn.

## Conflict Drives Plot

Conflict puts pressure on your characters to do something. This in turn propels the narrative forward, generating momentum. Tension can be external, pitting the protagonist against antagonistic forces and obstacles, or it can be internal, delving into the characters' inner struggles and contradictions. A good rule of thumb when writing is to make things hard on your characters. Then make them harder. If you ever feel like your story is lagging, take a step back and think about what hurdles you could put up in front of your characters.

## Conflict Builds Character

Conflict forces choices, and in doing so it illuminates a character's desires, fears, and vulnerabilities. We'll talk more about character development in chapter 4, but for now let's acknowledge that as characters navigate conflicts, they are often changed by their experiences. Without conflict, there is no transformation, and without transformation, a story risks feeling static and uninspired.

## Conflict Enhances Emotional Engagement

Readers become invested in characters' journeys when they share in their trials and triumphs. They rejoice in their victories, however small, and feel the sting of their defeats. This emotional investment is the cornerstone of a compelling narrative. It transforms passive readers into active participants, emotionally involved and intellectually engaged.

> Slow down where it hurts.
> —STEVE ALMOND

Have you ever heard the advice to write what you know? I used to squirm whenever I heard it because some of my favorite stories are rooted in richly imagined worlds that don't exist (think *Lord of the Rings* or *The Name of the Wind*). But what I've come to realize is that "write what you know" is actually great advice when it comes to writing the internal lives of our characters. We can all know our own emotions and it's worthwhile to write from that experience, even if it's not always pleasant.

In the next chapter, we're going to talk about another experience that can be unpleasant, one that we all deal with from time to time. It's the predicament of being unable to get words on the page, a phenomenon most people call *writer's block*. But I'm here to tell you that you never have to suffer from it again.

# PRACTICE & REFLECT

It's time to put theory into action. Here are some exercises designed to help you deepen your understanding and get comfortable leaning into the unfamiliar.

## OBSERVE YOUR DISCOMFORT (MEDITATION AND WRITING)

Set aside about forty-five minutes this week to experiment with the connection between physical and emotional discomfort. Check out SitWriteHere.com for guided meditations created specifically to help you sit with discomfort.

1. **Meditation** (ten minutes)
   - Sit comfortably and close your eyes. Set a timer for ten minutes.
   - Choose an anchor such as your breath, the feeling of your hands resting, or ambient sounds around you.
   - Stay still, resisting the urge to move, shift, or adjust unless absolutely necessary.
   - Notice any physical or emotional discomfort that arises.
   - Observe your reactions with curiosity. How does your mind respond to discomfort?
2. **Writing Exercise** (thirty minutes)
   - Immediately after meditating, spend thirty minutes writing about an uncomfortable emotional experience you've had.

- Go slowly and gently. Observe how your body and mind react as you write. If it becomes too uncomfortable, pause briefly and take a few deep breaths, then return to the page or, if you feel overwhelmed, stop at any point and move on to the next step.

3. **Reflection Questions** (five minutes)

    *After finishing your writing session, reflect:*

    - How did mindfulness affect your experience of revisiting discomfort?
    - Did observing your discomfort change your perspective on the experience?
    - What insights about yourself or your story arose during this exercise?

## EXPLORE YOUR AVOIDANCE

Write down the types of scenes, themes, or emotional states you typically avoid in your writing. Why do you think that is?

___________________________________________

___________________________________________

___________________________________________

___________________________________________

___________________________________________

___________________________________________

___________________________________________

___________________________________________

___________________________________________

___________________________________________

Reflect on how exploring these avoided areas could enrich your stories. Choose one and brainstorm ways you might gently begin writing into this discomfort.

## KINDNESS CHECK-IN

Over the next week, pay attention to your inner voice during your meditation and writing practice. Keep a small notebook nearby, and whenever you catch yourself being harsh or judgmental, take a minute to consciously replace the judgment with a kinder perspective and write it down. Notice how this simple shift in internal dialogue impacts your comfort level and productivity.

# THE MYTH OF WRITER'S BLOCK

A few years ago, I arrived at a retreat center in Mexico to teach a weeklong workshop, and the owners of the retreat center welcomed me with a tour of the campus. I made a mental note of a beautiful little spot where a coffee bar was set up for early risers, claiming the alcove near the fireplace where I envisioned writing each morning before I started teaching. But as the sun came up the next day, I quickly came to understand that this charming spot was where the morning hikers gathered before hitting the trails. It was bustling with friendly (oh so talkative) people at 5 a.m. I got very little writing done.

When my alarm went off on the second morning of the retreat, I had the thought, *Ugh, I don't want to go write.*

That might have been the end of it. It would have been so easy to just go back to sleep. Thankfully, the thought raised a little red flag. Writing in the early morning, enjoying a cup of coffee and a bit of quiet, is one of my favorite things. So I asked myself, "What is it I'm REALLY avoiding?"

It took me all of three seconds to realize that what I actually didn't want was to be social so early in the morning. I love people, but not before I've had my coffee. I knew if I went to the same spot I had gone the day before, everyone would want to say good morning and chat. I wanted quiet.

Once I realized that, it was easy enough to make it happen. Instead of going back to sleep, I swung by the dining hall to fill my coffee mug, then found a secluded place on the patio to do my writing, looking out over the blooming yucca. It was a beautiful way to start the day, and I got some good writing done.

Recognizing why you don't want to write is a critical skill to develop as a writer, because you never know when you might find yourself avoiding the work. I don't know a single writer who hasn't carved out precious time to write and then found themselves vacuuming their car or doing their taxes.

All writers have periods of time where they avoid writing. It's what most people call procrastination or sometimes *writer's block*. What a term. It's so final, so insurmountable. "You might as well just quit now and go do something else, you've got writer's block." Nonsense. Groundskeepers don't get mower's block. Stockbrokers don't get trader's block.

## IT'S NOT WRITER'S BLOCK

Once, when I was at a dinner party with my husband, someone asked me how I deal with writer's block, and I told them that I don't believe in it. My husband called me out. "You get stuck all the time," he said. And he was right. I do. Just the night before I had flopped down on the couch next to him and complained that I couldn't figure out what needed to happen next in my story. I was stuck. Getting stuck is part of writing.

It happens, but it's not "writer's block." The label matters because it obfuscates any possible Right View of the situation.

What I've learned over my many years of writing and working with writers is that "writer's block" is just a catchall phrase we use to say, "I'm having trouble getting any writing done." I don't use the phrase because the oversimplification acts as a kind of wall. It's a sort of mysterious term that evokes all kinds of superstition around writing that I just don't subscribe to.

The research backs me up on this. Study after study has shown that writer's block is actually a tangle of anxiety, perfectionism, emotional overload, lack of structure, some combination of those, or even (sometimes) all of them at once.[*]

When it's time to write and you notice you don't feel like writing, ask yourself why. Get curious about what's going on in your brain. Why are you resisting something that (on some level) you in fact really want to do? Is the house noisy? Are you not sure where to start your story? Are you feeling discouraged? Don't let yourself off the hook with an answer like "I just don't feel like it." Some part of you wanted to write badly enough that you set the intention to do so. Honor that part by digging in to find the real reason you're resisting the act of sitting down to do the work.

## Practice Makes Progress

When you meditate regularly, you gradually get really good at recognizing the thoughts that float through your mind until it

---

[*] For a more in-depth look at the underlying causes of procrastination and "writer's block," check out the work of Ronald T. Kellogg, Robert Boice, and Kalina Christoff Hadjiilieva.

becomes second nature to you. It's a practice that builds mental strength. In fact, you can think of practicing mindfulness meditation like lifting weights at the gym. I've never (ever) been excited to repeatedly hoist heavy dumbbells overhead. What I do love is getting home from the store with a trunk full of groceries, loading up five bags on each arm, holding a gallon of milk in each hand, and still having enough strength left over to raise one arm up and close the hatch.

Mindfulness meditation makes our minds strong for all the quotidian challenges we face, including the times when we don't feel like writing.

Start with the simple meditation practice from chapter 1 and find a way to do it regularly. This will require some discipline at first, until the practice becomes a habit, but it will get easier as you go along. To build new habits, two things are extremely helpful.

The first is called *habit stacking*, and it's the simple act of pairing the new thing in your life (in this case meditation) with something you already do regularly.* When I first decided I wanted to write in my journal every day, I paired the activity with my morning coffee (an already long-standing part of my morning routine). Years later, when I wanted to make a habit of meditation, I decided to take just ten minutes after I was done with my morning coffee / journaling routine. I would close the journal, set a timer, and be still for a bit.

Consider what habits you already have that you could stack with your new meditation routine. Maybe you meditate after

---

* *Habit stacking* is a term popularized by James Clear in his book *Atomic Habits*. It's a great read for anyone looking to establish new routines.

brushing your teeth, before crawling into bed. Maybe you could carve out a few minutes after lunch every day. Experiment a little and find what works for you.

The second way to support yourself in creating new habits is through community. In chapter 6 we'll talk more about the power of including other people in your mindful writing journey, but for now, I'll just plant the seed: Sharing your goals, having accountability, and surrounding yourself with a structured support system can make all the difference in building the life you want.

Once you've practiced meditation for a bit (the timeline will be different for everyone, but the more you practice, the quicker you will notice changes), you'll start to observe that you're more aware of your thoughts "off the cushion," that is to say, as you go about your everyday life.

For instance, you might notice the inclination to skip your writing time and do something fun like fold laundry, at which point you can pause and ask yourself why. In my experience, the noticing is the hardest part. If you can get to that point of reflection, of probing just a little deeper into the initial thought of *I don't feel like it*, it takes all of a few seconds to realize what's really going on inside your head. Maybe you don't know what happens next in your story, or you're feeling burned out, or your inner critic has been hard on you lately. Then you have a concrete challenge you can address.

## MEDITATION: EXPLORING AVERSION

If it's time to write and you don't feel like it, or if you find yourself avoiding the work, take ten minutes to practice the Insight Meditation from chapter 1 and then ask yourself why you're avoiding your work.

1. Set your timer and sit in a comfortable position.
2. Choose an anchor to rest your attention on, a place to bring your mind back to when it wanders (because it will).
3. After about five minutes, turn your attention toward the question of why you're avoiding your work and just notice what thoughts come up. What you will inevitably discover is that there's always a reason you don't feel like writing.
   - Maybe your children are being noisy and you need quiet.
   - Perhaps you don't know how to start your story.
   - It could be that you're feeling discouraged or unsure of yourself.

Once you know what that reason is, you can assess it and, instead of just succumbing to "writer's block," decide how to *act*.

   - Send the kids to the park for an hour.
   - Jump in at your second chapter and come back to write the first one later.
   - Read a book on craft, or take a course.

As soon as you have the answer you need, you can either end the meditation or continue to sit until the bell rings, because hey, you're already meditating, why not finish it out?

With a little mindfulness meditation practice under your belt, you'll be able to recognize when you're stuck, to pause and consider what's really going on, to strip away all the noise and get down to "just this," to recognize the past conditioning and/or present moment conditions that are actually preventing you from writing.

In my experience, the most common culprit is the inner critic.

It is almost guaranteed that, as a writer, you will have to deal with your inner critic. Most writers I know negotiate with it every time they sit down to write, whether they realize it or not.

## RECOGNIZING THE INNER CRITIC

If you've ever had the experience of writing a sentence/paragraph/chapter and then deleting it because it wasn't good enough, you've experienced what it's like to be paralyzed by your inner critic.

You could also call your inner critic your inner editor, because that inner persona is really good at seeing anything (and everything) on the page that isn't good enough. Your inner critic can be really useful when it's time to revise (more on this in chapter 5), but when you're working on a first draft, it will shut you down hard and fast if you let it. And it can be difficult to recognize.

When writers come to me and say that they're stuck in a cycle of deleting and rewriting, they don't realize that they're dealing with their inner critic. Some will even insist that it's not an inner critic. It's not like they actually hear a little voice in their head critiquing their work, but when I gently push them and ask "Why are you deleting and rewriting?" what we usually find is that there's some part of them that feels the work isn't good enough. They just have a deep sense of needing to make it better before it can exist. This is your inner critic trying to protect you.

You can think of your inner critic like a slightly high-strung but loyal pooch, dutifully defending you from danger. The problem is: Everything is a threat. That dog will bark at a squirrel outside the window, someone passing by on the street, or the sound of a door closing somewhere in the building. Much like that dog, our minds are dead set on protecting us, and even when we recognize that, and tell it to please be quiet, it's probably still going to bark. Thankfully, we can train our minds with meditation, and it's generally easier to do than training a dog not to bark.

The first thing to recognize is that when you write something, you are putting your thoughts and feelings on the page. It's a vulnerable act. It opens you up to criticism. For most of us, our earliest writing experiences were in grade school, and the feedback (intentionally or not) wasn't always kind. Your inner critic is focused on protecting you (always), whether it's from a wild tiger or unkind comments, and it does such a good job that it can sometimes shut you down entirely.

You can't edit a blank page.
—JODI PICOULT

I have a vivid memory of my dad reading something I wrote in fourth grade and chuckling. I hadn't intended the story to be funny, so I asked him why he laughed. He shook his head and said, "Your spelling."

He wasn't intending to be mean, but my dad was an excellent speller, and he was baffled by my inability to grasp the nuances of *i* before *e*.

Still, I felt ashamed, and it stuck with me. I continued to write, but kept it to myself in my journal. For a decade I thought I couldn't be a writer because I was a terrible speller. Writing anything that would be read by someone else made me anxious because I knew I would misspell something and it would open me up to ridicule.

By the time I was in my twenties, spell-check had become ubiquitous (and I have leaned gratefully on it since then), but that inner voice couldn't let go. My inner critic's warning, *If you write, someone will laugh at you*, was so well ingrained it didn't matter that I had the aid of those red squiggly lines on the screen alerting me to misspellings. I would not have told you that I had any hesitation based on that experience with my dad, it wasn't conscious, but every time I sat down to write, that self-criticism manifested as a generalized anxiety. When I started meditating, noticed that anxiety, and turned toward it, I realized the fear was around anyone reading my first drafts, so I decided very early on that no one would read my first drafts. That way, when the anxiety arose, I could just notice it, remind myself that no one was going to read it until I was good and ready to share it, then keep writing.

When our inner critic is so ingrained that it's no longer a little voice but a general physical sensation (like anxiety), there are really only two ways to deal with it.

You can go the unhealthy route and repress, repress, repress. This turns writing into a struggle, makes it crazy hard, and leads you to drink and smoke and stuff your face (sometimes all at the same time) to try to quiet that awful feeling that what you're writing is crap.

Or you can learn (by practicing meditation) to notice how you feel and the thoughts that run through your head when you sit down to write. Keep in mind that your inner critic is just trying to protect you. Always. It's on your side, it's just a little overzealous. When it whispers, *Wow, that sentence was terrible, you better delete that before anyone sees it*, please know that it's just trying to keep you safe from outside voices that might be hard on you.

The unavoidable truth is that, even when your work is all polished up and ready for publication, there will still be haters. No book is universally liked. Don't believe me? Go to Goodreads.com, look up your favorite book, and scroll down to the 1-star reviews. There are always 1-star reviews. Even for really good books.

We'll talk more about how to let criticism roll off your back in chapter 6, but for now just understand that there will be haters. You don't have to listen to them. You certainly don't have to worry about them before you've even finished your first draft.

The best way to deal with your inner critic (whether it's a distinct voice or a general sense of unease) is to give a little internal bow and say, "Thank you for trying to protect me, I recognize that's not the most brilliant sentence ever written, but this is just a first draft, I'll come back and make it better later." Or if you're feeling a little less Buddhist, maybe something like, "Yeah, yeah, shut up." Then just keep writing.

Now it's time to talk about what happens when your inner critic becomes particularly demanding, entrenched to the point that you don't even recognize it. You simply know that you cannot be responsible for producing anything less than flawless prose, meticulously crafted sentences, and captivating narratives right from the start.

This inner-critic-on-steroids is more commonly referred to as *perfectionism* and it can be utterly paralyzing, leaving writers unable to put pen to paper or fingers to keyboard. The fear of writing anything less than a masterpiece (as a first draft) becomes an insurmountable roadblock to progress.

> In order to do something well,
> we must first be willing to do it badly.
> —JULIA CAMERON

In the past, I thought of perfectionism as an outward expression of unrealistic expectations, because it's simply unreasonable to expect your writing to be perfect as you write your first draft (or ever, really), but over the years I've come to understand that the reason perfectionism is so disruptive to the writing process is not because it sets impossible benchmarks. Instead, it has to do with the fact that you're trying to constantly negotiate with your inner critic (your inner editor), engaging and then excusing it, over and over again, as you write.

Perfectionists are easy to spot because they struggle more than anyone else to write a first draft. They work on their outlines endlessly and have extensive character dossiers. They do everything but write the thing they want to write, and no matter how many times I insist that the first step is to simply get words on the page, they cannot allow themselves to write anything that isn't outstanding work the moment it hits the page. When they do manage to write, they labor over every word of every sentence, making painfully slow progress or (more likely) no progress at all.

Here's the crux of it: Writing and editing are two totally different activities. They require you to engage different parts of your brain. Creative writing is primarily associated with divergent thinking, which allows for the free flow of ideas, imagination, and narrative construction. The main brain regions involved include the

- prefrontal cortex, linked to self-expression, idea generation, and spontaneous creativity;
- default mode network (DMN), active when you are daydreaming or imagining new scenarios;
- hippocampus, responsible for memory retrieval;
- limbic system (including the amygdala), involved in processing emotions; and the
- temporal lobes, involved in language processing and understanding narrative structures.

Editing, on the other hand, requires convergent thinking, a more analytical and logical process that focuses on structure, grammar, and coherence. The brain areas activated during editing are the

- dorsolateral prefrontal cortex, crucial for logical decision-making;

- anterior cingulate cortex, which plays a role in error detection and conflict monitoring;
- left frontal lobe, responsible for language production and syntax;
- left inferior parietal lobule, involved in reading comprehension; and the
- executive control network (ECN), which allows for high-level cognitive functions like organizing, structuring, and critically assessing written content.

The transition between creative writing and editing involves shifting from the DMN (imagination, storytelling) to the ECN (logical analysis, error correction). If all these terms are overwhelming, think of having a writing hat and an editing hat. Now recognize that you can't wear two hats at the same time.

Let me repeat that: *You cannot write and edit at the same time.* It's multitasking, and science has definitively shown that multitasking doesn't work. You may think that you're writing and editing at the same time, but really what you're doing is engaging your writing brain for a bit, then shifting to engage your editing brain for a few seconds or even a few minutes to critique and polish up that sentence, only to reengage your writer brain to write the next sentence and then realize that actually that sentence doesn't work very well with the previous one and you're back to editing again. It's exhausting.

Some writers do work this way. I'm not saying it's impossible, but it's tiring and slow, and most writers who try to work this way end up quitting. It's tragic.

Writers who don't relish being hard on themselves learn to separate their drafting and editing processes, allowing creative ideas to flow freely before engaging their critical mind. This ties back to the playfulness we talked about in the "You Might Notice . . ." section in chapter 1. First drafts should ideally be an extended form of play. Allow yourself to explore and meander on the page. Which leads me back to the idea of allowing yourself to write a crappy first draft.

Let's be clear about a few things:

- No one ever gets to see it unless you decide to share it. Password protect the document if you need to reassure yourself of this, or if you have nosy roommates. Your crappy first draft is yours alone.
- The crappy first draft is also (more lovingly) called the *discovery draft*, for good reason. You want to slip into that state of creative flow when you're writing because it will allow ideas to come to you that you haven't even considered yet. When you try to edit as you go, you can only write what your analytical brain is focused on and you shut yourself off to the potential surprise of new ideas.
- That "crappy" first draft might not be as crappy as you think it is (remember your human tendency to look for the negative). So let's all agree to call it a discovery draft from here on out. The thing you have to learn to accept is that it's not perfect. No first draft is perfect, but done is better than perfect every damn day.
- It does get easier. My first drafts these days are way better than my first drafts were when I first started writing. I still don't let anyone read them. Not even my husband, who is the first person to read anything I write. He doesn't see my first drafts. He sees the second, sometimes even the third draft.

So how do you give yourself permission to write a less-than-perfect discovery draft? By noticing whatever little voice inside your head is insisting on perfection, then inviting it to take a seat and shut the hell up.

## THE CRITIC'S COMPANIONS

While our inner critic is almost always loitering nearby, waiting for an opportunity to jump in and make us doubt ourselves, there are other, very real reasons that we sometimes avoid our writing.

In my work with clients (and in my own experience) I've noticed that there are in fact eleven things that can sometimes masquerade as "writer's block." The inner critic may top the list, but it is by no means alone.

1. The Inner Critic
2. Fear of What People Will Think
3. Burnout
4. Medical Challenges (for you or loved ones)
5. Distraction
6. Writing in the Wrong Format
7. Unrealistic Expectations
8. Material Is Too Fresh
9. Overwhelm
10. Not Knowing What Comes Next
11. The Story Isn't Yours Anymore

I explore each of these in depth in the appendix starting on page 166. When we strip away the myth of "writer's block," what's left isn't some mysterious affliction but a set of understandable, workable challenges. Sometimes it's distraction, sometimes perfectionism, sometimes plain old fatigue. The point is: There's always a reason, and if you can pause long enough to ask yourself what it is, you can take action instead of shutting down.

To address each of the above challenges in full, I've created a guide at the back of the book called "Reasons We Sometimes Avoid Our Work." There, I've included detailed, practical suggestions for how to notice and push through everything from burnout to not knowing what comes next, but it all starts with getting quiet and asking yourself what's really keeping you from your work.

Writing will never be free of resistance, but with practice you can learn to meet that resistance with curiosity instead of surrendering to it out of fear. Some days that means negotiating with your inner critic; other days it means recognizing that life has simply gotten in the way. Either way, you are not broken, and your writing is not doomed. You just need to find your way back to the page, and that is a manageable task.

◆

## PRACTICE & REFLECT

Consider what's really keeping you from writing. If you've carved out the time but continue to avoid the work, review the list in this chapter and get really honest with yourself.

- Is the material too fresh?
- Are you afraid of what people will think?

- Are you feeling burned out?
- Are you (or a loved one) feeling unwell or do you have a new baby in the house?
- Are you distracted?
- Are you writing in the wrong format?
- Have you set unrealistic expectations for yourself?
- Is your inner critic making things hard on you?
- Are you overwhelmed?
- Are you not sure what should happen next in your story?
- Is the story still yours to write?

If after looking over the list that starts on page 166 you're still not sure, take some time to meditate (five to fifteen minutes) and then ask yourself the question again. Remember there's no wrong answer. What's more, your experiences are private. You don't have to tell anyone what has you feeling blocked. The invitation is to be deeply honest with yourself. Writing in a private journal can also be revelatory. Explore, on paper, what you're feeling when you're avoiding your work.

With a little practice, it becomes easier to see through the veil of "writer's block." Then you can address whatever it is that's in your way and get back to work.

4

# TIME FOR A GUT CHECK

We're about halfway through the book at this point, and I feel compelled to take a quick time-out and ask an important question: Have you been reading along but skipping the exercises, meditations, and writing prompts? You don't have to raise your hand or anything. The question isn't meant to shame you. We all have books that we've bought, read, and put on the shelf without taking any action whatsoever, but I'd like to point out that if you don't actually do the work, you won't experience any of the benefits.

So it's time for a gut check.

If you haven't taken any action yet, pause for a moment and ask yourself why. Try to get down to the real honest truth of "just this" in this moment, right now. What are you experiencing?

Perhaps you need to slow down and give yourself more time to reflect and practice the meditations between chapters. Maybe it's an issue of logistics. If you're reading this book in bed or listening to it in the car, it might not be practical to meditate right this second. If that's the case, make a plan for when you're going to try adding a meditation to your writing time. Just like you're going to make time for your writing, you can make time to start meditating before you write.

If the challenge isn't logistical, if you find yourself thinking that all this sounds interesting and you'll give it a try "someday," consider that you might be coming up against some internal resistance. Resistance is part of the creative journey. Recognize it, turn toward it, and get curious.

What are you getting out of staying blocked? Sometimes there are hidden rewards to remaining stuck.

- Security: If you never risk writing, you never risk being vulnerable.
- Superiority: You can laugh at or judge those who dare to put themselves out there.
- Martyr status: You can say you were "too busy" being the better parent, partner, or employee.

This isn't about blame. It's about choice. So be kind to yourself. You can think of yourself like a character in a story. You're facing some internal conflict, and that's a good thing. As we've discussed, conflict is what pushes us to grow and change. It presents us with choices. The opportunity is to choose something new, to do things differently than you've always done them before.

If you want a freer, fuller, more creative life, this is your invitation to commit.

Take a breath.
Check in with yourself.
Then do something to make a change in your life.

5

# THE POWER OF EMOTIONS

If you don't like talking about emotions, you're not alone. They're messy things. Unpredictable. Powerful. But if you can acknowledge that and lean into your newfound ability to get comfortable with discomfort, you'll find that exploring your emotions (and the emotional motivations of your characters) will help you write beyond simple archetypes to create individuals that feel real to the reader.

> A good plot is always necessary,
> but what really grips the reader is character.
> —DONNA TARTT

It's true for nonfiction "characters" as well. One of the biggest challenges in writing memoirs, biographies, and other historical accounts is finding the emotional angle. Without an understanding of what motivated the people in a story, the book becomes a tedious recitation of facts. But if you can impart to the reader why the players did what they did, you invite understanding and compassion, which in turn engages the reader to care more deeply about the outcome of the story.

The best way to start exploring emotions is with yourself. Meditation creates opportunities for you to notice and then understand the feelings that are driving your behaviors (either consciously or subconsciously). The more you understand this for yourself, the broader and richer the palette you will have at your disposal when creating your characters. Writing convincing individuals requires you to feel what they feel. Then (and this is the hardest part) you have to stay with those emotions long enough to capture them on the page.

This is challenging work. No joke. And you will benefit from having established a regular practice of meditation before you engage in the deeper work of exploring emotions. This might mean taking a week or two to practice the meditations I've introduced in previous chapters before reading any further. Or it might mean reading through this chapter but waiting to do the meditations I've included here until you've got a little more experience with the basic practices from the first half of the book. Give yourself permission to move through the material in whatever way, and at whatever pace, feels right to you.

## HOW TO EXPLORE EMOTIONS

There are three effective ways of exploring emotions in an effort to capture them on the page. The first, and the easiest, involves making a lot of silly faces.

For almost forty years now, scientists have been studying how you can evoke emotions by simply changing your facial expressions and posture. If you want to feel sad, google an image of a sad face, do your best to replicate it, pay attention to how you feel, and you will very likely notice sadness. It's not foolproof, but a 2019 meta-analysis[*] found that this does, in fact, seem to work, that your emotions tend to follow cues from your body.[†] If you want to write a happy character, smile. If you're working on a scary scene, put yourself in a fabricated flinch.

This might explain why writers so often move around or pace the room as they're trying to figure out a story. Sometimes finding the physical stance that seems appropriate to a situation can help you feel its corresponding emotion. Then, once you're feeling what your character would feel, you can use your increasing tolerance for discomfort to stay with the sensations long enough to put words to what you experience, get those words down on the page, and understand how the emotions dictate your character's next actions. This is a fairly easy, if superficial, way of exploring emotions.

To step things up a notch, you can use the focused space of meditation to evoke specific emotions. Say you're writing a character who has a broken heart. You can engage in a state of deep focus to explore the experience of heartache as a researcher might, using your ability to sit with discomfort to get curious, to note the physical sensations and emotional reactions that occur.

---

[*] A *meta-analysis* aggregates the results of lots of studies on the same topic into one big study. This technique can reveal trends that may not be obvious in a stand-alone study.

[†] For more information on this, check out Nicholas A. Coles, Jeff T. Larsen, and Heather C. Lench, "A Meta-Analysis of the Facial Feedback Literature: Effects of Facial Feedback on Emotional Experience Are Small and Variable," *Psychological Bulletin* 145, no. 6 (2019): 610–51, https://doi.org/10.1037/bul0000194.

## MEDITATION: EVOKING SPECIFIC EMOTIONS

To intentionally explore specific emotions during a meditation, start by doing ten minutes of traditional Insight Meditation focused on an anchor. This will ground you and give you a place to return to (mentally) if the emotion begins to feel overwhelming. Then, when you're ready, you can intentionally recall a time when you felt that specific emotion.

1. Set your timer for fifteen minutes.
2. For the first ten minutes, simply focus on your anchor, coming back to it when your mind wanders.
3. When you're ready, intentionally bring to mind a time when you felt the emotion you wish to explore. Really revel in the memory and notice how it feels in your body. It will likely be unpleasant, but just see how long you can be with it.

As soon as the timer goes off (or you feel like you've had enough), take a deep breath and end the meditation.

Write down everything you can remember about the physical sensations associated with the emotion. You will almost certainly overwrite the descriptions. That's okay. You can come back later to edit it all down and choose the best line or two. (We'll talk more about the editing process in the next chapter.)

*A quick reminder about self-care:* If at any point this practice feels like it's draining or like it's too much, let it go. You can always come back to it another time, or with the help of a therapist. Take care of yourself and go at your own pace.

## Somatic Meditation

Both of the above methods are good at exploring a specific emotion for the purpose of writing about it, but there's a third way of exploring emotion that is much more powerful. It's called *somatic meditation.*

There is a growing body of research supporting the idea that emotions and memories are not solely processed in the mind but are also stored and expressed in the body.[*] Somatic meditation combines the principles of somatic therapy with mindfulness meditation and involves deep, body-focused awareness.

Remember back in chapter 2, how I said there are only a few ways you can do meditation wrong and they mostly have to do with retraumatizing yourself? Tapping into deep, powerful, often unrecognized or traumatic emotions can be really overwhelming if you don't go about it carefully and with assistance. If you have any unresolved trauma in your background, or even if you're unsure, I strongly suggest that, before you do a self-guided exploration of somatic emotions, you find a therapist, ideally one trained in mindfulness-based stress reduction (MBSR) or eye movement desensitization and reprocessing (EMDR).

---

[*] To learn more about somatic experiencing, check out *The Body Keeps the Score* by Bessel van der Kolk and *Waking the Tiger: Healing Trauma* by Peter A. Levine.

That said, as long as you're feeling steady emotionally, you can try somatic meditation. The main difference between this meditation and the previous one is that with somatic meditation, we're not attempting to evoke any particular emotion. Instead, we're simply scanning the body with open awareness, getting curious about whatever arises.

## SOMATIC MEDITATION: NOTICING YOUR OWN EMOTIONS

To explore your own emotions, start by nurturing an open awareness with a basic Insight Meditation. When you're ready, you'll turn your attention to the physical sensations of the body with kind curiosity and just see what presents itself. Because it includes two parts (cultivating open awareness followed by exploration), this practice takes a little more time. I recommend starting with twenty-five minutes. (I have recorded a guided meditation for exploring emotions on my website at SitWriteHere.com.)

1. The first step is to identify emotional sensations. Start with the basic Insight Meditation described in chapter 1, noticing thoughts that arise, letting them go, and coming back to the anchor. After about ten minutes (it can be helpful to set a timer), turn your attention inward and scan your body for any pronounced physical sensations, usually in the front of the torso, neck, throat, or face. It can take a while

to notice these sensations, so be patient. Eventually, you might notice tightness, or warmth, or tingling. When you notice something, get curious. Is there an emotional component to it? There might be. Or there might not. You might notice your stomach rumbling and realize you're hungry. That's fine. But if you turn your attention to a tightness in your chest and suddenly notice sadness arising, you have tapped into some stored emotions.

2. The next step is to explore. When you notice a specific emotion, and if you feel steady, turn your attention toward it. Investigate with curiosity. You might label it with whatever word comes to mind, for instance: sadness. Then try to stay with it for a few seconds and check in again. Does it still feel like sadness or has it shifted into something else? Get curious about it and ask yourself, "What is sadness?" What does it feel like? With no stories built up around it, just in this moment, right now, what are you experiencing?

3. When you feel like you've explored the emotion even a little bit, try to write down what you've experienced. The point of this exercise is twofold: You're learning to explore emotions from a strong steady base, then practicing the art of putting words to those feelings.

4. Sometimes the experience of somatic emotions will not be as clear-cut as what I described. Perhaps you notice a sensation in your neck or jaw, but it doesn't seem to be connected to anything in particular. It doesn't "feel" like any specific emotion. In that case,

just label the actual sensation: tightness, warmth, or even "something." If it's unpleasant, you can label it that: "unpleasant." Then, again, get curious. Does it change as you bring your attention to it? "More unpleasant" or "less unpleasant" or maybe "tightness" may turn to "aching." Try to be present with it, as it is, moment to moment, using your writerly skills to label it as specifically as possible. Sit with it for as long as is comfortable (or maybe even a little uncomfortable), then come back to your anchor. You can also put a hand on your heart, or open your eyes to ground yourself back in the here and now.

Remember to be kind with yourself and go slowly. This can be tricky work.

In truth, what often happens when difficult emotions arise is that your mind, sensing the impending discomfort and wanting to protect you from it, will throw other thoughts at you. You may notice a deep sense of sadness and then realize you're drafting an email you're going to send when you're done meditating. When you notice that you've gotten distracted, you can thank your mind for working so diligently to protect you, then recenter on your anchor and, when you're ready, open your awareness again to whatever sensations are present. You might notice the same sensation as before, or you might notice something different. You might not feel anything. Every moment is unique and what rises to greet your conscious mind is unpredictable.

When discussing emotions, what is most often reflected upon are the difficult ones (anger, anxiety, sadness), but those are not the only emotions that can come up in meditation. It's important that you know this. If you keep up your meditation practice, you will have sits that are blissful, full of satisfaction and joy. They can be quite lovely. While there can be some challenges around not clinging to those experiences, the bigger challenges you will face, as a meditator, are around dealing with the difficult emotions, the unaddressed traumas of your life, both big and little.

## Examining Emotions

All this, the joyful sensations and the difficult ones, can be used in your writing. We'll talk about how to integrate these explorations into your work, but first there are a few key things to understand about examining emotions and trauma specifically.

In the mindfulness context, you can think about trauma in terms of big-T trauma (death of a loved one, war, severe injury) and little-t trauma (every other pain or disappointment in life). The tendency to dismiss little-t traumas is understandable, especially in the face of so much big-T trauma happening around the world, but your body carries those little t's around, same as the big T's.

Depending on how you were raised, there may have been emotions that were not acceptable for you to express. Say, for example, you were taught (like most of us) that anger is an unacceptable emotion and so every time in your life that you felt it, you had to keep it to yourself, bottle it up. Those bottled-up emotions are stored in the body. Suppressing and controlling these emotions actually takes a lot of energy.* Someone says something that pisses you off, but instead of feeling it, expressing it, and dealing with it, you ignore what you're feeling, push it deep down inside, and it just stays there, like a vampire, sucking up energy you need to do all the things you love.

It doesn't have to be a big-T traumatic event for it to get logged in your tissues. What's more, science is learning that the conditioning you carry in your body might not even originate in your own lifetime.

You probably learned, back in high school biology, that with rare exceptions, your genetic code doesn't change. Your DNA is replicated and passed down from generation to generation, but what scientists are learning now is that the genes are just the code. How that code is translated is something else entirely. This is *epigenetics*, and epigenetic expression can change in response to stimuli.

Imagine your DNA is like a giant instruction book for your body. It tells your cells what to do, like what color your eyes should be or how tall you might grow. In this metaphor, epigenetic markers are like little sticky notes added to the book. The sticky notes don't change the actual words in the book (your DNA), but they tell your body which parts to read and which parts to ignore.

For example, let's say your DNA has instructions for curly hair. Epigenetics can add a sticky note that says, "Don't read this!" and you might end up with straight hair instead. You can think of epigenetics as the way a body decides which in-

---

* For more information on how suppressing emotions can sap your energy, see the work of James Gross, Roy Baumeister, and Daniel Wegner.

structions to use and which to ignore, depending on what's happening in your life. These sticky notes can be added or removed, and they can be passed down to your kids.

A 2013 study looked at the intergenerational effects of trauma in mice. At the start of the study, the researchers repeatedly filled the mouse cages with the smell of cherry blossoms, then zapped the feet of the mice with an electrical current, just enough to cause a jolt of pain. The mice were thus trained to fear the smell of cherry blossoms.

Then, the offspring of these mice were raised with other mice (who had not been conditioned to fear the smell of cherry blossoms) in cages that had no electricity in the floor. They had a totally normal upbringing. What the scientists found was that when they exposed those offspring to the smell of cherry blossoms, the mice got jumpy and nervous. It's interesting to note that the fear centers of their brains weren't triggered in the same way as their parents', they were simply more sensitive to the trigger. When the scientists dissected the brains of the offspring, they found more neurons in the specific region involved in detecting the smell of cherry blossoms, as compared to control mice.* This carried through generations. Two, three generations down the line, the descendants of those mice still had a heightened sensitivity to the smell of cherry blossoms.

I share all this to try to remove any sense of blame or shame you may encounter around big feelings. Maybe you had a perfectly happy childhood, and yet you still feel like you're carrying around deep emotional pain. This can cause a whole secondary level of suffering because, you tell yourself, "What do I even have to complain about?" You might start to feel like there's something wrong with you.

My hope is that understanding the science behind stored trauma might free you from trying to figure out why you feel what you feel, and instead just acknowledge it. Take heart in the fact that all those big feelings might not even be yours. You might be triggered by something that was associated with trauma in your grandfather's brain, decades before you were born. The good news is that, even if the trauma didn't originate with you, it is within your power to unravel it, and the trick to doing so is awareness. You can process the trauma you're carrying by acknowledging your emotions, sitting with them, and allowing yourself to feel them.[†]

To picture how this works, I like to use a metaphor from the world of chemistry. If you combine sodium bicarbonate

---

* It's a fascinating study: Brian G. Dias and Kerry J. Ressler, "Parental Olfactory Experiences Influences Behavior and Neural Structure in Subsequent Generations," *Nature Neuroscience* 17 (2014): 89–96, https://doi.org/10.1038/nn.3594.

† If you'd like to know more about this kind of trauma therapy, check out Peter Payne, Peter A. Levine, and Mardi A. Crane-Godreau, "Somatic Experiencing: Using Interoception and Proprioception as Core Elements of Trauma Therapy," *Frontiers in Psychology* 6 (2015), https://doi.org/10.3389/fpsyg.2015.00093.

and acetic acid (also known as baking soda and vinegar) all at once, you get a foamy explosion. It's possible you played with this reaction as a kid when you built models of volcanoes. If you did, you might have noticed that if you add only a drop or two of vinegar, you don't get much of a reaction.

You can think of your emotions as the baking soda, and your awareness as the vinegar. If you try to sit and open up to all your emotions at once, you will get an explosion of some kind, and it will likely be intensely unpleasant. But if you just touch into your emotions, if you just bring a drop of attention, you'll get a little fizz that quickly settles down. This is *titration*, the process of adding one substance to another very slowly and carefully so that you can control the reaction.

Every time you touch into a strong emotion, even if only for a moment, you are allowing it to be expressed so that it no longer has to be stored in your body, and when you're no longer trying to hold all your emotions deep inside, you can write about them more easily, without losing your shit.

I'd like to invite you, the next time you need to write a scene that depends on difficult emotions, to remember this practice of mindful titration. With it, you can touch into big emotions gently, sit with them for as long as you're comfortable (or maybe even slightly uncomfortable), and use that time to write about them. Then, when something starts to feel explosive or overwhelming, you just come back to the anchor until you feel settled and calm. Then touch into it again if you feel able, or you might wait for another day, or you might decide that you want a therapist to guide you through this after all.

Tread carefully. The last thing you want to do is poke too hard at old wounds. Take care of yourself. There is no blue ribbon for toughing this out on your own.

## YOUR OWN EMOTIONAL THEMES

As you become more aware of your emotions, you open a rich vein of thematic material that can inform and deepen your narratives. What you will likely find is that you're drawn to certain ideas that resonate with your worldview, experiences, and the messages you wish to convey through your work, including questions about human nature, society, love, loss, and redemption, to name a few. This thematic inclination is a natural part of the creative process, and as you delve into exploring emotions, these themes will emerge in your work more distinctly, which will allow you to use them in your writing with more intention.

However, while you're working on your first draft, I suggest that you don't spend a lot of energy thinking about themes. Nothing makes a piece of writing feel more clunky than an author pushing motifs into a story. For at least one draft, just write. It's nearly impossible to recognize themes in incomplete work. The very definition of a theme is a recurring idea. You have to give it time and space to recur. Once you have a draft and you read through it, then it makes sense to look for themes, but if you don't immediately recognize them, be patient. It can be difficult to see your own patterns of thought. That doesn't mean they're not there.

Every writer has ideas that they circle back to repeatedly, whether they realize it or not. It took me years to recognize my own affinity for certain subject matters, but looking back it's easy to see how, in my earlier work, my characters all deal with abandonment in one way or another. In the larger context of my life, this isn't too surprising.

When I was growing up, my dad was dealing with a pretty

intense case of PTSD from his time in Vietnam in the 1960s, and he really couldn't stay in one place very long. He was always leaving, taking jobs in other parts of the world, disappearing for months, sometimes years. It was not unusual for me over the course of my childhood to end my day getting tucked in by my dad and wake up to find that he had left in the night with no indication of when he would be back. As a little girl, I felt abandoned and heartbroken every time he left. Of course, as an adult and a parent, I have a much better understanding of the terrible internal suffering that motivated my dad's actions (and I'm beyond pleased to say that he and I have grown close in my adulthood), but the stories I wrote before becoming more aware of my own emotional landscape are largely centered on those feelings of abandonment.

In my first novel, the women are stoic and strong, each of them dealing with unacknowledged feelings of abandonment in their own way. It worked well for that story, but when I started my next project and found myself more or less writing the same characters, I decided I wanted a wider variety of emotions to work with.

Only after recognizing my own themes was I able to intentionally write characters who have different emotional backgrounds. These days, when I find myself writing a character motivated by fear of abandonment, I pause, then choose whether to embrace that theme or push past it. Because if all my characters have the same fear, my stories will all, on some level, be the same. With more awareness comes the ability to choose. I can choose to model a character on someone else I know well and use their issues, their emotional background. These days, I try to give my characters issues that clash. For instance, one with a fear of abandonment falls in love with another who fears commitment (talk about instant conflict!). But it all starts with awareness of emotion.

## WRITING BELIEVABLE CHARACTERS

Heroes, sidekicks, mentors, and villains—these descriptions are all relative and completely dependent on who is telling the story. This is important to keep in mind when you want to create well-rounded individuals who come across as real people. As the author, you need to understand what has happened to your characters in their lives (a collection of events usually referred to as backstory) so that you can write convincing, unique individuals who will resonate with readers on a profound level.

If you write characters into a story without understanding their emotional motivations, simply to fulfill a role, you run the risk of your narratives becoming predictable, boring, and transparent.

Consider the villain.

The concept of an inherently bad person, or someone acting out of sheer malevolence, is not only unrealistic, it's also uninteresting. A villain who is bad "just because" will predictably do the worst thing at every turn, but a character who has a complex web of emotional motivations will be difficult to predict, making them much more interesting and giving you, as the author, more options for how your story plays out.

As always, there are exceptions. If you're writing a thriller about someone who is psychologically detached from basic human experiences like empathy, you might have a character who is inherently "just bad," but as a general rule, no one is a dick "just because."* When people are cruel, it is almost always because cruelty was modeled for them, and they don't know any other way to get what they need. When you stop to explore why your villain is such a rotten person, you will almost certainly find some interesting backstory.

Likewise, a main character who is good "just because" is not very interesting. How did they learn to be strong, or kind, or clever? What life experiences shaped them into who they are?

It's also worthwhile to keep in mind that no one is all one thing. A villain might be nice to animals, and a hero might lie to protect someone's feelings. Life is full of gray areas. The nuanced emotions that motivate their actions are what makes a character feel complex, interesting, and ultimately human.

## Finding the Emotional Core

The best way to get to know your characters (fictional or not) is to play a little game I picked up from my kids when they were toddlers. I call it "Ask Five Times Why." When you ask why five times, you start to get to the emotional core of motivation.

Start by picking a scene in your story and choosing one character to focus on. What do they do in this scene? Why do they do it? Once you have that answer, ask again. Why? Then again. And twice more. At each step, just let the answers come. Sometimes writers feel uneasy making things up, but that is your job as a writer (and bonus: it's super fun). You can always change your mind later, but first see what your instincts tell you.

---

* Even though psychopathic characters are detached from emotions like empathy and guilt, they still have a very real internal logic. They generally believe they are rational and justified, and it is essential, when writing a character like this, to get inside that skewed but coherent worldview.

As an example, let's consider a surprise birthday party being hosted by a middle-aged man, we'll call him Phil, for his wife, Phoebe.

### ASK FIVE TIMES WHY

1. Why did Phil decide to throw this party for her? Because he loves her and wants her to feel special on her birthday.
2. Why does he want her to feel special? Because she's been feeling down about getting older. He wants to cheer her up.
3. Why does it matter to Phil? (Don't answer why she's feeling down about getting older, pursue why it matters to Phil.) He is afraid that in the face of their inevitable decline and ultimate deaths she will give up on life, stop taking care of herself, and just fall into an easy chair for their remaining years together.
4. Why does he fear that? (Again, we're not asking why she would do that, we're investigating why Phil fears it.) He doesn't want to lose her as a partner. He has big dreams for their retirement that include her.
5. Why is he afraid of losing her? Phil's mom died when Phil was young, and his dad gave up on living, fell in his La-Z-Boy, and watched TV for forty years, basically ignoring Phil, who felt lonely for most of his life until he met Phoebe.

By the time you get to number 4 or 5 you start to get some interesting backstory. Phil's mom died when he was young. His dad didn't handle it well. Phil was left feeling lonely and abandoned. Once you've unpacked these basic ideas, put your creative mind to work and imagine a little more. What city did all this happen in? What did mom die of? How did dad pay the bills? These are the things you need to know about your character.

Some writing coaches will tell you that you need to know everything (and they mean everything) about all your characters. The internet is full of insanely long questionnaires you can fill out, listing your protagonists' favorite ice cream, their shoe size, their most beloved childhood toy, and so on. The energy spent on those questionnaires could be applied to your writing and the truth is, you don't need to write down every detail about your character. If you get to a scene where you need to know something simple, like Phil's favorite flavor of ice cream, just pause and make something up. You're a writer. Trust your gut.

On that note, I always recommend giving your gut a fair amount of credence in the process of writing. You'll notice that this whole "Ask Five Times Why" exercise starts with the character doing something. Maybe you had an outline, maybe you just wrote the scene without knowing why. Either way, great work! For your first draft, your gut will serve you just fine.

Once you have a draft, you can go back to dig deeper into the reasons behind the scenes you wrote on instinct. When you do, consider that all character motivations are emotional at their core. And since motivations are what drives action, it's easy to draw a direct line from emotions to plot.

## A QUICK NOTE ON PLOT

We don't have a ton of space in this book to dissect plot, but I will take a minute because it is so tightly woven with character emotions. Here's everything you need to know about plot in one, wildly oversimplified sentence: Somebody wants something, so they _________, but then _________, so they _________, but then _________ (repeat as necessary, increasing the stakes as you go) until the character gets what they want (or they don't).

Notice that it starts with someone who wants something. Desire. Desire is one of the most powerful emotions we have.

To take this even one step deeper, consider that emotions are spurred by your perceptions. If you perceive that someone is angry with you (even if they're not), certain emotions will arise that are likely to prompt certain actions.

When you take the time to understand the emotional landscape of your characters, you're no longer just crafting a series of events. You're weaving a narrative that grows out of the characters themselves, making for a story that's cohesive, dynamic, and deeply human. Working this way, you may find, as you get to know your characters better, that your story morphs and changes. That's to be expected, because your plot should always give way to character.

This is the number one reason I always hold my outlines loosely (if I write them at all). When I'm outlining my stories, I generally have not yet fully explored my characters' emotional lives. As I start to write, I come to know them better (by questioning their choices five times), and I must be willing to change the plot to remain faithful to who these characters are.

As an example, let's say I have my character come to a literal crossroads in a small town. To the left is a gym. To the right is a carnival with candy apples. I may want my character to go left. I might even need her to go left because that's where she meets her workout godmother and learns to do a proper burpee, which is how she gets strong enough to be victorious in the final battle. But if I've written a character who loves sweets and roller coasters, that gal is going to turn right, every time. If I have her turn left, the choice will read as inauthentic and the whole story will start to feel contrived.

Of course, this is a ridiculous example, but hopefully you can see how it would apply to a metaphorical crossroads in your story (the choice of which love interest is the right one, or which job offer to take). Emotions (desire, fear, loneliness, anxiety) are the driving force behind the decisions your characters make, and they determine the actions your characters will take, and thus propel the story forward.

Emotions are at the very heart of your story. It's worth taking the time to explore them.

## PRACTICE & REFLECT

Take some time to practice and integrate these insights into your own writing process.

### PRACTICE THE MINDFULNESS OF EMOTIONS MEDITATION

You can follow these steps on your own or use the guided version available at SitWriteHere.com.

1. Begin with Insight Meditation (ten minutes)
   - Sit comfortably and settle into your breath.

- Practice the basic Insight Meditation described in chapter 1, anchoring your awareness on the breath or another steady point of focus.
- When your mind wanders, gently bring it back.

2. Body Scan for Sensation
    - After ten minutes, shift your attention inward.
    - Slowly scan your body, especially the front of the torso, neck, throat, and face.
    - Notice any physical sensations (tightness, warmth, tingling, tension, etc.).
    - Be patient. Let sensations arise on their own time.

3. Get Curious
    - When you notice a sensation, pause and get curious: *Is there an emotion here?*
    - If it's a neutral cue (like hunger), just notice it.

4. Name the Emotion (if one is present)
    - If an emotion arises, label it gently: *sadness, anger, grief.*
    - Stay with it for a few breaths.
    - Ask: *Has it changed? Is it still sadness? Or is it something else now?*
    - Let it shift and evolve without trying to fix or solve it.

5. Stay with the Sensation (if no clear emotion is present)
    - If the sensation doesn't link to a clear emotion, just name what *is* there: *tightness, pressure, warmth, ache,* or even just *"something."*
    - Use your writer's mind to describe it as precisely as possible.
    - If it's unpleasant, name that, too: *unpleasant, sharp, dull.*

6. Be Present with It
   - Watch the sensation moment by moment. Does it intensify? Soften? Shift in shape or location?
   - Keep your attention there gently, with compassion.
7. Return to Your Anchor
   - After a few minutes, or when you feel complete, return to your breath or anchor.
   - Rest in that stillness before ending your meditation.

## TRY THE SAME MEDITATION TO EXPLORE YOUR CHARACTER'S EMOTIONS

This exercise is an adaptation of mindfulness meditation to help you safely explore and inhabit your character's emotional landscape.

1. Set aside thirty minutes.
2. For ten minutes, practice Insight Meditation by focusing on your breath or chosen anchor to settle your mind.
3. For the next ten minutes, choose one emotion your character experiences deeply (fear, sadness, longing, anger, etc.). Imagine yourself fully in your character's shoes during a pivotal moment when they experience this emotion.
4. Notice the physical sensations arising in your body as you embody this emotion. Gently remain present with the sensation (or end the meditation if it feels like too much).
5. For the last ten minutes, write freely about this emotion. Capture its physical sensations, thoughts, and

how your character might act from this emotional state.

REFLECTION QUESTIONS:

What did it feel like to embody your character's emotions?

_______________________________________________

_______________________________________________

_______________________________________________

_______________________________________________

_______________________________________________

_______________________________________________

_______________________________________________

_______________________________________________

Did this experience offer you deeper insight into your character? How?

_______________________________________________

_______________________________________________

_______________________________________________

_______________________________________________

_______________________________________________

_______________________________________________

_______________________________________________

_______________________________________________

## ASK FIVE TIMES WHY

This exercise helps uncover the emotional core driving your characters' actions.

Instructions:

Choose a key scene from your current project and focus on one character in the scene.

Why did they make the choice they did in that scene?

_________________________________________

_________________________________________

_________________________________________

_________________________________________

_________________________________________

Now dig deeper by asking *why* again.

_________________________________________

_________________________________________

_________________________________________

_________________________________________

_________________________________________

Ask *why* again. Take care not to jump characters.

_________________________________________

_________________________________________

_________________________________________

_________________________________________

_________________________________________

And again: Why?

_______________________________________________

_______________________________________________

_______________________________________________

_______________________________________________

_______________________________________________

Last time: Why?

_______________________________________________

_______________________________________________

_______________________________________________

_______________________________________________

_______________________________________________

After completing this process, write a brief summary (one or two paragraphs) about the emotional backstory that emerged.

REFLECTION QUESTIONS:

- Did you discover anything surprising about your character's motivations?
- How might these insights impact your story moving forward?

## PRACTICE "EVERYBODY'S THE HERO"

Characters come to life when you remember that each one believes they're the hero of their own story, even the antagonists. You can try the following exercise for one of your own characters, or choose one from a book or story you know well.

EXERCISE:

Select the antagonist or a secondary character.

Write a short paragraph from their perspective, explaining their motivations as if they are absolutely justified in their actions.

____________________

____________________

____________________

____________________

____________________

____________________

____________________

Reflect on how this changes your understanding of this character.

____________________

____________________

____________________

____________________

____________________

____________________

____________________

## EXPLORE YOUR OWN THEMES

This reflective practice helps you uncover personal themes that frequently arise in your writing.

1. Spend fifteen minutes reviewing your previous stories or writing in a journal about stories you're drawn to.
2. Notice if you find recurring themes or emotional patterns.
   - Write down what you find and reflect:
     Do certain emotional themes appear repeatedly in your work (e.g., fear, abandonment, loss)?

     _______________________________________

     _______________________________________

     _______________________________________

     _______________________________________

   - Can you identify experiences in your life that might be influencing these recurring themes?

     _______________________________________

     _______________________________________

     _______________________________________

     _______________________________________

   - Consider how being aware of these themes can either enhance or limit your storytelling. How might you choose differently next time?

     _______________________________________

     _______________________________________

     _______________________________________

     _______________________________________

6

# MENTAL FORMATIONS

In the previous pages, you've learned how Insight Meditation can help you tap into a focused state of flow and allow you to write with greater ease. You've explored mindfulness of emotion and even practiced sitting perfectly still to build your tolerance for discomfort. You've also investigated how awareness of thoughts can help you better understand the underlying causes of writer's block so you can maintain a regular writing practice. All this has been building on the principle of Right View, the wisdom to perceive reality without the distortions of your expectations, fears, or conditioning. But there's a deeper layer to this foundation.

Consider for a moment that your brain is not impartial or static. It is constantly taking in information through your five senses and interpreting it to make sense of the world around you. Everything that has happened to you in your life affects how you translate the reality of the present moment into thoughts, emotions, and intentions. Buddhists call this *mental formation*.

Mental formations are unique to every individual. They're the reason that the exact same circumstances can affect different people in different ways. Consider how a piece of modern art can inspire awe in one person and skepticism in another, or how a spicy dinner can be enticing to some and repulsive to others. It's all about mental formations and the causal sequences that generate them.

Imagine a woman, let's call her Julia, who was taught from a young age that being skinny was of the utmost importance. She was often praised for skipping meals and on the rare occasion she did indulge in sweets her stepmother would have her stand on the bathroom scale and shame her by saying in a mocking voice, "I'm so proud of you." Decades later, after receiving a prestigious award at work, Julia's friend exclaimed, "I'm so proud of you!" and came in for a hug. Julia found herself suddenly frozen in place, overcome with feelings of disgrace and guilt. Emotionally and physically, because of her own mental formations, she was reacting to being humiliated. Thankfully, Julia was a practiced meditator. She knew that while her initial reaction was understandable given her past experiences, it wasn't useful in that instance. She was able to take a breath and see clearly that her friend was genuinely excited for her.

When it comes to writing, you can take care to notice how your own mental formations can deceive you while at the same time nurturing the mental formations of your readers, layering in all the juicy details that will gently lead them to see the settings, hear the dialogue, and draw the conclusions and revelations you wish to share with them through your stories.

## OUR OWN MENTAL FORMATIONS

When I was working on my second novel, I had the idea to open the story with the birth of the main character during a terrible storm. In my mind, I pictured lightning and thunder, wind thrashing through the trees, and big, fat raindrops hitting the mud in little explosions. The whole thing felt wonderfully dramatic. I wrote the scene and then continued writing until I finished the draft. Then, I came back to the beginning to start my revisions. I remembered choosing this dramatic storm to open my story, but when I read the start of the first chapter, what I had actually written was this: "It was raining."

Um . . . that didn't quite capture it, to say the least.

What astonished me was that I hadn't noticed, on the first pass, that all the details were missing. They only existed in my head. When I had written "it was raining," I imagined all the wind and rain and mud, but none of that was on the page. Those were all mental formations evoked in my mind by those three words.

When we read our own work, it's very easy to let our minds fill in the blanks, but if it's not written down, it won't make it into the minds of your readers. Recognizing this, I took a day to rewrite the entire first scene with all the dramatic elements I had originally intended. It was much better when I was done because all the powerful details were actually on the page. (Side note: I ended up cutting the whole chapter to come into the story later. #writerslife)

Before I became aware of how my own mental formations could lead me astray, my writing process for any given project was lengthy and often frustrating. My first book went through twelve full drafts over eight years because I would write it and then have someone, usually my very patient husband, read it and give me notes on what wasn't working, and then I would rewrite.* Nowadays, when I read my own work, I catch 90 percent of the things that still need development. By recognizing what exists only in my head and what's there on the page, my revisions can focus more on exploring new, expanded possibilities for the story. I do far fewer drafts. My work simply gets better faster.

The key here is to notice the details. Slow down and mindfully consider each piece of information. Ask yourself, "Is it on the page?" If not, write it down. Your story will be better for it.

## A SERIES OF DISCOVERIES

Now let's consider how you can use the concept of mental formations to build out imagined realities in the minds of your readers. It's really quite remarkable how starting on page one, your printed sentences are transformed into elaborate imagined realities in the minds of your readers. The human brain is constantly predicting, layering, and updating meaning based on every detail it encounters. That means your words don't just land once. They ripple out.

As you guide a reader through a story, you're not simply

---

* Here I feel compelled to point out that spouses are not always the best choice when you're looking for feedback. I'm lucky to have a partner who is also a writer, and we've spent two decades developing a way we talk about story, so we can be honest about what's not working and still love each other at the end of the day. Tread carefully. Hiring a professional to give you feedback is worth every penny if it saves your marriage.

informing, you're shaping how they interpret what comes next. Each detail, each image, each word quietly trains their brain to anticipate more of the same. The mind, after all, doesn't reset with each new sentence. It accumulates, filters, and recalibrates, moment to moment.

Think of the reader's attention like a beam of light in a darkened room. With your sentences, you direct that beam, choosing what gets illuminated and what stays in shadow. The story unfolds not all at once but as a series of guided discoveries. And with each one, you reshape the reader's understanding of what the story is and where it's going. You do this in three ways:

1.  Physical descriptions: You put your readers in the scene and begin to build their mental formations by specifically describing the physical details of the world and the characters in it.
2.  Character behaviors: You introduce readers to the specific quirks and foibles of your characters so that the plot unfolds in a way that feels inevitable.
3.  Emotional explorations: By writing authentic emotional experiences, you help your readers form an empathic bond with your characters and share in their triumphs or defeats.

Let's take a look at each of these in turn.

## Physical Descriptions and Transcending Cliché

Well-crafted descriptions draw your readers in by helping them to envision a fully formed reality, but what makes certain descriptions engaging while others fall flat as clichés? To address that question, you have to understand what a cliché is.

Evolutionarily, our brains are wired for efficiency. When faced with a challenge, whether physical or linguistic, we reach for the easiest solution. It's not laziness; it's human nature. So, when you try to describe a shade of blue, the first thing that pops to mind might be "sky blue." It's familiar. Fast. Automatic.

This is exactly how mental formations work. Over a lifetime, we gather impressions, phrases, and imagery that form well-worn paths in the mind. When we encounter something new, the brain doesn't start from scratch. It filters incoming information through everything we've seen and heard before. That's why we reach for clichés like "fire-engine red" or "soft as a pillow." These phrases are shortcuts, deep grooves carved by repetition.

But here's the problem: Because they've been used so many times, they carry the weight of countless, unpredictable associations in the mind of the reader. A cliché can't possibly land cleanly. The mental formation it triggers will be clouded, tangled up with other stories, childhood memories, even advertising slogans. When you rely on cliché, you outsource your imagery to the reader's mental formations. Instead of conjuring a vivid image, the word or phrase dissolves into noise.

To be clear, clichés are not a grand failing on your part as a writer; they're just a result of how the human brain is wired, and frankly, clichés are fine for a first draft. They serve as excellent placeholders. When you're just getting started with a story, go ahead and use all the clichés you need to get the words on the page. But when you come back to revise, consider what can be gained by slowing down and mindfully setting an intention to truly observe, to engage deeply with your settings and consider how your characters would perceive them.

For example, let's say that in your first draft you have your character sit down beneath a big tree. With the words "big tree" you've basically created the literary equivalent of clip art in your reader's mind (picture two parallel lines with a bouncing scribble at the top). "Big tree" does the job, sure, but it's a missed opportunity. Pause for a moment and be mindful of the details. Consider each of the five senses. As your character nestles their bottom between the swollen roots of a craggy oak, let them feel the rough bark, hear the birds singing, and see the dappled light fall through the canopy of tiny, waxy leaves. Suddenly, the reader is there, immersed in the scene. That's the power of seeking out specific descriptions.

And they don't have to be verbose. Consider the difference between a character wearing a red dress and that same character in a scarlet gown that clings to her like a second skin.

The latter doesn't just tell you the color of her attire; it gives you insight into the character's confidence, her desire to stand out—all in only a few words.

The trick to transcending cliché is detail. It's the mindful attention to the unique aspects of a scene that elevates it from mundane to memorable. Finding those perfect, descriptive details is work. It's the work of being a writer. You must strive to see beyond the obvious, to depict the world not as it's been described a thousand times but as it is in that moment. That's where you find the descriptions that begin to create a unique experience in the minds of your readers.

As another example, let's say you're writing a scene about a character who walks into a kitchen and has a fight with her mother. What do you picture? What does the word *kitchen* evoke in your mind? Do you picture gleaming countertops and white recessed-panel cabinets?

Or do you picture a room that could maybe use some attention, with dishes piled up and trash that needs to be taken out?

Or maybe you picture rustic brick walls and a coffee per-colator on the stove, with a view of a farm out the window?

Hopefully you can see how *kitchen* means something dif-ferent to every reader. What's more, the specific details of the kitchen in your story will influence how the reader imagines the scene. Take a moment to picture the mother and daughter who live in each of the kitchens I've described here. You can tell readers a lot about these two women without talking about them at all, just by describing the kitchen.

Same for cars. If you write that your main character gets in their car, you have missed a chance to tell me about this person. A teenage boy who gets in a beat-up 1998 Honda Accord is a different teenager from one who gets into a shiny 2025 Tesla.

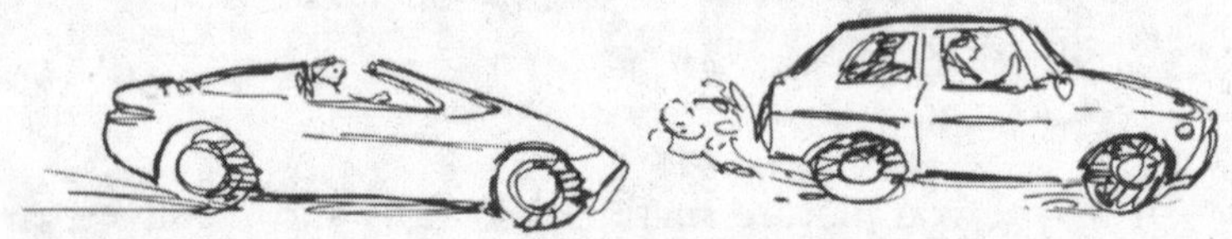

Details like these guide the reader in their understanding of your fictional world and the characters in it. When you read through your draft and come across something that could conjure a multitude of images in a reader's mind depending on their particular background and conditioning, do your best to notice this and ask yourself, "Is there an opportunity here to be more specific?" If so, rewrite to give those details. By taking the time to layer in significant details, you become a more intentional author, guiding the reader in forming their understanding of your imagined world and the characters in it.

## Character Behaviors

In chapter 4 you learned how to explore the deeper emotional lives of your characters with the goal of creating distinct individuals. As you're writing, try to stay attuned to why your characters do what they do. Consider that every character's behavior emerges from their unique mental formations, which are shaped by their backstory, traumas, beliefs, and emotional conditioning. As authors, we can create deeper, more resonant characters by understanding and honoring the mental formations that drive their decisions. Are they behaving in a way that aligns with their established traits and emotional state, or are they being steered by your desire, as the author, to move the plot in a specific direction?

It's a strange paradox, but as an author, one of your most important tasks is often to get out of the way. You spend so much time imagining these characters, imbuing them with rich backstories and complex emotional lives. Then you need to let them act authentically. This means allowing their actions to unfold in a way that respects their emotional journey, even if it means deviating from your planned trajectory. This authenticity is what makes characters resonate with readers; it brings them to life in a way that is both believable and compelling.

The more you practice meditation, the better you will get at noticing when something doesn't land quite right. If you find that the character you've created is taking your story so far off track that it's no longer the story you want to tell, you can change their backstory. For instance, if you need your character to be bold at a pivotal moment to take your story in the direction you want it to go, you can tweak their upbringing to give them an intrepid streak. Give them a mentor or friend who models courageous behavior. When you layer in these types of elements, you are building the mental formations in your reader's mind to understand how, even if your character starts off meek, they have the potential for daring action, but you have to strew those breadcrumbs along the path.

If you read something you've written and you get that little niggling sensation at the back of your mind when you ask yourself, "Would they really do that?" Stop. Notice that sensation. It can be quite subtle, but as you practice mindfulness, you will get better at recognizing the quiet part of your brain that knows something's off. Novice writers dismiss that intuitive nudge. They know something isn't right, but they dismiss it with the hope that no one will notice. Make no mistake, readers will notice. Even if you can't immediately discern what exactly about the prose isn't working, circle that section so you can come back to it.

A good way to work through character motivations is to freewrite in a journal. Write as if you're the character reflecting on the scene. What do they want? Why are they doing what they're doing? Go back to chapter 4 and do some of the exercises there to help you explore their deeper motivations. Then, once you're feeling really solid in what's driving them, jump back a few pages in your manuscript and read the scene again, looking for whatever it is that doesn't align with what you now know about your characters, and adjust as needed to create authentic actions that fit your characters' understandings of the world (their mental formations). This is how you create narratives that unfold in a way that feels natural and true.

## Emotional Responses

When you read through your draft, set an intention to mindfully notice what comes up (or not) in your own mind and body as you're reading. This practice builds on the work we did in chapter 4. If you find yourself getting teary or excited as you read, you're onto something powerful and probably don't need to edit much, if at all.

If, however, you read something that you intended to be emotional but feel nothing, notice that. It's a hint that you need to add more details. Sometimes this means going all the way back to the beginning to consider how you can build up to the emotional response you want to evoke. Layer in the plot points that will allow the reader to build mental formations that will pay off later in the book.

In stories, as in life, mental formations are the result of experiences. Emotions don't arise from plot twists alone. They emerge from a sequence of experiences, each one laying the groundwork for the next. You can take advantage of that fact and give readers the experiences they need to understand the story as you intend them to.

For example, if you write that a character suddenly realizes she's in love, the words are likely to ring hollow. To convincingly write a character falling in love there has to be a progression of scenes that establish interest and build attraction. The infatuation needs to have a spark and manifest physically with a quickening heartbeat and a flutter in the belly, then progress through the phases of attraction, maybe spurred on by a kiss, or a note of endearment that causes them to be distracted. When a character who has been experiencing all these things suddenly realizes she's in love, the reader will be right there with her, feeling the excitement and joy of a budding romance.

When the emotion you're seeking to evoke is one that is generally considered unpleasant (heartache, fear, anxiety), this can be particularly challenging. If you find yourself skimming over sections that are difficult to write, revisit chapter 3 and continue practicing with discomfort. It does get easier.

## CHOOSE WISELY

Whenever I teach about layering powerful details into your writing to guide readers on a journey, someone always raises their hand to say that they would rather write stories that are fast-paced and easy to digest, even if it means the writing fails to evoke certain images or feelings. They don't want their book to become a slog, mired in excessive details that test the reader's patience. They often share this comment with a bit of smugness, as if they've caught me giving bad advice, so it's always fun to agree with them.

We've all read books that indulge in endless, unnecessary descriptions or emotional verbosity. I have certainly been known to flip through a few pages to get back to the plot (or put a book down entirely) when I find myself reading paragraph upon paragraph describing the finer nuances of fabrics (or tools or physics), or when the characters' emotions are explored in prolonged reflections.

The art of embedding compelling details into your writing isn't about padding your prose with fluff. Each detail you include (or omit) shapes the mental formations of your reader. Good writing isn't about piling on more; it's about choosing the right details to guide your reader's interpretation. Using your own understanding of how the mind collects input to build imagined realities, you can choose which details to include, and which to let go.

The balance between brevity and depth is crucial. Readers appreciate a story that moves swiftly and avoids unnecessary detours. They also enjoy the richness that well-selected details can bring. By carefully choosing how to describe both your settings and your characters, you can craft narratives that are engaging and evocative, ensuring that your writing resonates deeply without collapsing under the weight of too many descriptions.

> A line will take us hours maybe / Yet if it does not seem a moment's thought / Our stitching and unstitching has been naught.
> —WILLIAM BUTLER YEATS

This is perhaps most challenging when writing emotionally complex scenes. Often it can take a few tries to figure out exactly what you want to say about a character's internal state, and so your first drafts can sometimes feel like they circle around emotions, like water swirling a drain, before you finally land on the thing that you really meant to say, the thing that truly captures what you envisioned in your mind and felt in your body.

Here, too, editing comes down to balance. Try to notice which sentences give new information and which give the same information in different ways. When you find two sentences that say about the same thing, see if you can cut one, or condense them into one, more powerful sentence. Then take a break, come back, and read it again while noticing what emotions you feel in response. Then do it again.

This takes time. Allow yourself that time and keep working on your scenes until they capture exactly what you intended to portray. To speed up the process, you can learn to become more aware of how mental formations influence both you as the author and your readers.

## BE YOUR OWN BEST EDITOR

When you finish a draft, print it out, tuck it lovingly away in a drawer, and let it rest there for as long as possible, ideally a month. During this period, shift your focus to a different project, or read as many books as you can by others. This effectively allows you to forget the intricate web of details and narratives you've been so deeply entangled in.

Then, when you're ready to open the drawer and begin editing, the first thing to do is invite your inner critic to step forward. In chapter 3 we talked about how, when you're working on a first draft, the inner critic can undermine your confidence and shut down your creativity. It's important in those early stages to quiet that part of your brain, but when it comes time to edit, the inner critic's natural inclinations toward judgment make it a top-notch editing partner, scrutinizing your work for inconsistencies, superfluities, and areas lacking clarity or impact.

### MEDITATION: INVITE YOUR INNER CRITIC TO THE WORK

To engage your inner critic as a writing partner, start with five to fifteen minutes of Insight Meditation to heighten your awareness of whatever thoughts or physical sensations might arise as you read through your draft.

1. Find a comfortable place to sit.
2. Set a timer for five to fifteen minutes.

3. Close your eyes if you wish. Take a few deep breaths. Choose an anchor for your attention, a place to come back to when your mind wanders.

4. When the bell rings, open your eyes and read your work. Pay close attention to questions such as:
   - Do the physical descriptions show the reader what you're picturing in your mind?
   - Is this character behaving in a way that aligns with what you know about them?
   - Do the emotions in each scene unfold as a natural progression of everything that has come before?
   - Do you notice any physical responses in your body as you read through sections that were meant to be emotional?

Embrace this opportunity for your inner critic to shine. Just remember that engaging your inner critic while editing doesn't mean succumbing to negativity or self-doubt. Instead, adopt a mindset of constructive criticism, where the goal is to challenge your work to be its best version. Listen to that critical inner voice, but maintain confidence in your creative vision. If you find your inner critic is getting the upper hand, try to take a half step sideways into discernment. Instead of telling yourself, "This is terrible," try asking, "Is it working?"

Mark Sarvas, one of my favorite writing teachers, always leads his instruction with conventional wisdom around writing (things like not starting your story with a dream sequence), but is quick to add that writers should do what's right for their own stories. When a student wants to try something wacky with their story, he might advise against it but always adds, "Hey, it works if you can make it work."

But how do you know if something is working? Your writing has to satisfy only two requirements to be considered "working":

1. Readers aren't confused.
2. They keep reading.

If your readers are still reading and they understand what's happening in the story, you can feel confident that your story is "working," and you can make that determination for yourself, before ever letting someone else read your work, by mindfully engaging your inner critic.

Let's look at the example of starting your story with a dream sequence. The main reason this is traditionally discouraged is that the first pages of your novel draw a reader in and introduce them to the characters/setting/stakes of the story. Dreams can be confusing by their very nature, so by starting with one you run the risk of befuddling your readers straightaway. But even if the dream isn't confusing, at some point your character has to wake up and readers tend to be frustrated when they learn that the characters/setting/stakes they've become invested in over three, ten, or even forty pages weren't "real." If you read through your dream sequence opening with your inner critic mindfully engaged, you're more likely to notice that the sudden paradigm shift might confuse your readers and cause them to put the book down. Then you can edit in whatever way will best keep them from being discombobulated.

Once your story is "working" on this most basic level, everything else is a personal preference. Here, too, mindful discernment is key. What do you like in a story? What bugs you? And where do you start if you don't even know?

I had a meditation teacher once who told a story about hitting a very low point in his life. He didn't know what he wanted in a relationship or work or anything. He felt like he didn't even know what he enjoyed anymore.

His own meditation teacher suggested he walk to the store, buy two types of apples, eat them, and decide which one he liked better. The next day, he would buy the preferred apple and a third kind and again, decide which he liked better. He was to do this until he had tried every apple the store had on offer, until he knew what kind of apple he preferred. Then he would have one thing he knew he enjoyed. I think about this story a lot. I think about him tasting each apple, comparing it to the other one he bought, thinking about what he liked or didn't like about each one.

We can do this with writing, too. If you write poetry, buy yourself a collection of poems, read two, and choose the one you like better. Then read another and compare it to the previous winner. Which of those do you like better? Keep going until you've read every poem in the book and have a favorite. Then put some thought into what you liked about it. Be as specific as you can. When you're reading a book, pause and notice your reaction to it. Are you enjoying it? Try to pinpoint why or why not.

It's important as a writer to have opinions, because creating art of any kind is just an extended process of making choices. Every step of writing requires you to make decisions based on your own preferences. Maybe you like high fantasy stories with intrepid heroes. Or perhaps you can't get enough of stories set in big cities told by charmingly neurotic protagonists. Or it could be you're excited by hard-boiled detective stories set in the 1940s. Mindfulness helps you to recognize your own reactions to stories you encounter as a reader, to notice the plots, themes, and archetypes you're drawn to. Then you can choose to lean into them, tweak them in interesting ways, or write something different entirely.

## NONATTACHMENT

Of course, the more you work on a project, the more emotionally invested you will become. This is perfectly natural, but it can also make it difficult for you to cut and revise effectively. This is where the Buddhist concept of *nonattachment* can be incredibly useful.

In Buddhism, nonattachment is the practice of relating to people, emotions, possessions, and ideas without clinging to them or needing them to stay the same. It's not about rejecting or avoiding the world; it's about being present and engaged without trying to control or possess.

When we can embrace nonattachment, we can write something with all our heart, not holding back, while also knowing (deeply knowing) that it will change. It might get edited, or moved, or cut altogether. There is great freedom in this.

When I was a kid, my sister and I built a sandcastle at the beach. It was glorious and we were very proud. Our cousin, who must have been about two, waddled up and, to our horror, proceeded to belly flop right into the middle of our masterpiece. After crying and complaining to our mom (who could do nothing to restore our sandcastle to its former glory) we decided to rebuild. We tried to keep our cousin away, but when we were about half done with the new castle, she broke through our defenses and again threw herself face-first into our work. On our third attempt, we had hardly begun scooping sand into place when she steamrolled the whole thing.

By then the tide was lapping at our first creation and we realized how fleeting the whole endeavor was anyway, so we began pushing sand into a mound, calling it a castle, and watching the glee on our cousin's little face as she destroyed it, laughing that contagious toddler's laugh. We detached from any concern regarding a finished sandcastle and had fun playing in the sand.

Writing is easiest when you let go of any attachment and just enjoy the journey. Accept that every paragraph you write, every sentence, is a little like a sandcastle with a conniving toddler looming over it.

Writing is hardest when you identify too closely with your work, when you see the pages you write as extensions of yourself. We'll talk more about this in the next chapter, but you are not your work. When you find yourself reluctant to cut a paragraph, ask yourself, "Does this bit of writing serve the story? Does it move the plot along or help the reader to understand my character? Or am I attached to it because I wrote it?"

If you've been practicing the Insight Meditations I've shared with you so far in this book, you're already practicing nonattachment. Every time you notice a thought and let it go, you're honing your ability to let all things rise and pass away. All you have to do now is recognize that you can apply that practice to your writing.

Most writers are familiar with the phrase "kill your darlings," often attributed to William Faulkner, who probably picked it up from Arthur Quiller-Couch, who lectured about writing in the early twentieth century. It's a suggestion to writers that they cut the sentences, paragraphs, and chapters they're clinging to like precious children. Why do you suppose this little snippet of advice is still batted around after so many years? Because it's something we all struggle with as writers. It's really hard to let go of any bit of writing you like, even when you know deep down (or not so deep down) that it no longer serves the story. When you know you should cut something but don't want to, it often manifests as a sensation of tightness in the mind or body. Mindfulness can help you to recognize this sensation. Then, once it's brought up into your conscious mind, you can see the vestigial writing for what it is: an opportunity to practice letting go.

The best way to nurture nonattachment to your writing is to have a file where you can put your darlings. Simply create a folder on your hard drive, call it "darlings," and put all the brilliant turns of phrase, scenes, or chapters that no long serve your story in there. This way you don't have to kill them. You just lovingly relocate them.

After years of moving snippets to my "darlings" folder, I started to realize that I had never pulled anything out of it. I still could, I suppose, but at this point I trust that whatever I come up with moving forward will be better than those darlings that didn't quite work for whatever reason. Embracing a "there's more where that came from" attitude helps a lot with nonattachment.

## PRACTICE & REFLECT

In this chapter, you've seen how mental formations influence your writing and your readers' experiences. Now it's time to practice engaging with them more directly.

### OBSERVE YOUR OWN MENTAL FORMATIONS

Understand how your past experiences and biases shape what you put on the page.

INSTRUCTIONS:

1. Choose a scene you've written.
2. Read it slowly, then write a brief journal entry describing what you *think* is on the page.
3. Now ask a trusted reader to read the same scene and describe what *they* understood or pictured.
4. Compare.

REFLECTION QUESTIONS:

* Where did your expectations and their interpretation differ?
* What mental formations shaped your original writing?
* How can you clarify or reframe to better guide your reader?

## CULTIVATING DISCERNMENT

Practice discerning what works in your writing by clearly identifying your preferences.

INSTRUCTIONS:

1. Pick up two novels you enjoyed recently. Identify a favorite scene from each. Write down specifically what you liked about them.

________________________________________

________________________________________

________________________________________

________________________________________

_______________________________

_______________________________

_______________________________

_______________________________

_______________________________

2. Now review a recent scene you've written. Can you recognize similar strengths in your work, or areas where you'd like to incorporate those strengths?

_______________________________

_______________________________

_______________________________

_______________________________

_______________________________

_______________________________

REFLECTION QUESTIONS:

- How does clearly identifying your tastes help you edit your own writing?
- What new insights about your storytelling preferences did you gain?

## EDITING WITH YOUR INNER CRITIC

Invite your inner critic to the table to offer constructive feedback.

INSTRUCTIONS:

1. Select a scene from your work that you feel is nearly finished.
2. Set a timer for thirty minutes and allow your inner critic to voice all doubts, critiques, and questions without censoring yourself. Write down each criticism in the margins or on a separate sheet.
3. After your timer goes off, shift your mindset to discernment. Review the critiques and choose three constructive changes you'd like to make based on the feedback.

REFLECTION QUESTIONS:

- Which of your inner critic's observations felt most valuable?
- How did shifting from criticism to discernment change your perspective on editing? Did it help you to see the work more clearly?

## DETAILED MINDFULNESS REWRITE

This exercise focuses on enriching your descriptions by observing details.

INSTRUCTIONS:

1. Select a short paragraph from your manuscript that relies on generic or vague descriptions (like "big tree" or "nice kitchen").
2. Spend a few minutes visualizing the scene vividly, noticing details you haven't explicitly described.

3. Rewrite this paragraph with richer, more precise details that intentionally guide your reader's mental formations.

REFLECTION QUESTIONS:

* How did mindfulness influence your ability to identify more engaging details?
* How does your revised paragraph more clearly guide the reader's imagination?

## NONATTACHMENT EDITING PRACTICE

Practice letting go to enhance your editing skills.

INSTRUCTIONS:

1. Copy a scene from your manuscript (around 1,000 words).
2. Edit this passage down by half. Aim for around 500 words. Cut and condense ruthlessly, removing everything that doesn't clearly move the story forward or deepen understanding of character or setting.[*]

REFLECTION QUESTIONS:

* Was it difficult to let go of certain sentences or details? Why?
* After editing, does your scene feel stronger, weaker, or simply different? Why?

---

[*] To be clear, I wouldn't necessarily suggest doing this for your entire manuscript (unless you want to). It's just an exercise to illustrate how much information you can get across using fewer, more intentionally chosen words.

# EQUANIMITY

Thus have I heard:* Before he found enlightenment, the man who would become the Buddha was a prince, living in luxury and wanting for nothing. When he left his castle and went in search of truth, he fell in with ascetics who renounced all worldly pleasures, barely eating or drinking enough to stay alive. After experiencing both intense luxury and harsh asceticism, Siddhartha Gautama recognized that true wisdom didn't come from the extremes. It resided in the middle. He called this the *middle path*.

---

* After the Buddha's death, his disciple Ānanda is said to have begun his recitations of the Buddha's teachings with "Thus have I heard," marking that he was faithfully transmitting what he had heard directly from the Buddha. I like it as a nod to the fact that these are stories that have been passed down.

To walk the middle path as a writer is to see yourself clearly in relation to your work. To do this you must first find *equanimity*, an internal composure from which comes great strength.

I like to think of equanimity as trying to balance marbles in the center of a plate that you hold in the palm of your hand as you go about your day. The marbles never really come to rest. They skitter about as you're jostled by big emotions, rolling around closer to the center as you calm down. If you get really out of balance, you run the risk of losing your marbles. They roll right off the plate.

The role of meditation, then, is to lift the edges of that plate, even if only slightly, so that your mental health is more like a shallow bowl. You might get pushed off-balance from time to time, the marbles may roll to one side or the other, but they don't go over the edge, and you can restore your equilibrium more easily. From this place of stability, it becomes much more likely that you will be able to persist in the pursuit of your creative goals.

## HOW TO PERSIST

Persistence is easy when everything is going well. When you're loving your story, and the words are flowing, and every door seems to be opening for you, you would be crazy not to keep going. But when the words slow down and the rejection letters start coming, when wave after wave of difficult times come at you, how do you keep your head up and carry on?

You can't stop the waves, but you can learn to surf.
—JON KABAT-ZINN

## Practice Non-Identification

The best way to persist is to put a little healthy distance between yourself and your writing. You are a writer, but you are not your writing. That manuscript you're working on? It is not you. You are not it.

This is called *non-identification*, and it is one of the core concepts in traditional mindfulness practice. It's similar to the nonattachment we discussed in the last chapter, but it's related more to being defined (or not) as a person by experiences or things. You can think of nonattachment and non-identification as two sides of the same coin: one reduces suffering by softening clinging, the other by softening ego.

Non-identification can be tremendously useful, and it's easy to practice. Try this next time you sit down to meditate: When you notice a physical sensation, like an itchy elbow, instead of saying to yourself, "My elbow is itchy," try rephrasing: "There is an itch." Or if you realize you're restless, try noting it in your mind so that it sounds something more like, *There is restlessness*. It makes it less personal. It's not your restlessness. You don't have to own it. It's just restlessness, one of countless normal human experiences that come and go. Notice it and let it pass like everything else in this world.

Once you have a little distance from your thoughts, you can make an honest assessment of their veracity. Where I find this to be most useful is with rejections.

Rejection is part of being a writer, and you all KNOW you shouldn't take it personally, but there's that little voice in your head every time you don't win a contest or receive a rejection letter or get a pass from an agent or publisher. That little voice that says, *Maybe I'm just not good enough.*

Start by noticing that thought. The more you practice mindfulness, the more easily you will be able to take that first critical step. Then, I'd like to invite you to do three things:

1. See clearly that you were not rejected, the writing was.
2. Embrace the uncomfortable reality that you have no idea why your work was rejected. Maybe the person who read it was having an off day. Perhaps it wasn't a good fit for that agent/publication/contest. It could be that your story was too long (or too short). Writing is an art and there will always be someone who doesn't like any given piece of art. It's just a fact.
3. Resist the urge to shoot yourself with the additional arrows of self-loathing, recrimination, and doubt. Try to let yourself feel the pain of the rejection without adding to it.

The reality of the publishing world is that most of the rejections you will receive as a writer will come without explanation. This leaves a mental void your inner critic is only too happy to fill, telling you that your work isn't good enough. And frankly, one of the reasons it's so hard to ignore is that it might occasionally be right. It's this possibility that gives your inner voice so much power.

Here's the good news: The quality of your work is the one factor you actually have some control over. Here again we revisit the concept of Right View. Take an honest look at what's on the page. Invite your inner critic to the party and ask the hard questions: "Is the dialogue natural, are the sentences or stanzas well worded, does the plot move the story forward?"

If it all looks good to you, but you have a gut feeling it could be better, there are things you can do to work on your craft. Take classes, enroll in workshops, read a book on writing, hire a coach.* As a writer you should always be learning, studying, and growing.

Keep it up and at some point, when you turn toward that little voice and ask, "Is my work really not good enough?" you may very well find that, actually, you're really proud of that piece of work, and it's entirely possible the rejection was because the piece was too long, or too short, or not a good fit for some other reason. Rejection really is a part of being a writer, but so is persistence. Keep writing, keep submitting.

When doubt does rear its head, think of it as an obnox-

---

* If you're looking for a coach/course/workshop, check out my website at aprildavila.com. I have a wonderful community of teachers and editors I work with. I can hook you up.

ious little cousin to the inner critic. Acknowledge it and then smother it with kindness.

## Push Aside Impostor Syndrome

If you stick with writing, you will eventually enjoy some success, whatever that means to you (finishing a piece, getting it published, or getting positive feedback in one form or another). Then you get to deal with impostor syndrome, another close cousin of the inner critic, which doesn't really pipe up until you start getting some positive feedback.

- You finish a draft of your project and that inner voice tells you not to get too full of yourself because people do this all the time. (For the record: they don't, and you should celebrate.)
- A story or poem you wrote gets published, and the voice sarcastically speculates on how few people will actually see it.
- An agent offers to represent your work, and the little voice insists she was probably having an off day; she won't be able to sell your book/play/screenplay.
- Your project is a wild success and your inner critic enthusiastically tells you that you just got lucky. "Wait till you try to write your next book/screenplay/collection," it says, "then everyone will see you're a fraud."

Point is, your inner critic (and all its obnoxious cousins) will NEVER run out of things to say. What's more, no amount of external validation will ever feel like enough if you don't find a place of internal satisfaction.

Success is not final, failure is not fatal:
it is the courage to continue that counts.
—WINSTON CHURCHILL

Write the words you feel called to write, to the best of your ability, and then be aware of those little voices sounding in your head. When you have moments of feeling discouraged, know that it's perfectly normal. Through mindfulness practice, you can notice the discomfort of these low points and try to sit with it. Think of the rejection like an itchy nose. Is it unpleasant? Yes. Will it be the end of you? No.

## KINDNESS AS A PRACTICE

Sharon Salzberg is one of the founders of the Insight Meditation Society in Massachusetts and author of the book *Lovingkindness*. In it, she talks about the difficulties of life being like salt, and how if you mix a tablespoon of salt into a cup of water and drink it, it's going to taste gross. But if you drop that same amount of salt into a much larger body of water, like a bathtub or swimming pool or a lake, it will be diluted to such a point that it's indiscernible. The salt remains the same, but the spaciousness of the container makes all the difference in how you experience it.

The salt in this metaphor represents all life's difficulties. As Salzberg points out, you have very little control over how much trouble you will face in your lifetime. What you can do is make your "container" more spacious so you can dilute any amount of salt that comes your way. So how do you do that?

*Loving-kindness meditation* (traditionally referred to as Metta) can be tremendously useful in helping to navigate life's challenges. Specifically, it helps balance out any negative self-talk that gets entrenched in your mind. Building on the mindfulness of thought practice from chapter 1, it works to push in positive statements to replace the negative ones.

With this practice, you can start to train your mind away from reflexive judgment and into a space that is much more open so you can see things as they really are.

Some people struggle with meditation, especially loving-kindness practice, because they feel it's self-indulgent. They don't believe sitting still and wishing themselves and other people well can create any tangible good in the world. But consider this: As you go about your day, when something happens that would normally irritate you or prompt you to say something snarky or mean, if you've been practicing kindness, repeating phrases like "May you be happy," you are more likely to respond to the irritant with kindness. Science backs this up.

A 2011 study showed that even short-term training in compassion practice increased prosocial behavior.[*] In short, people who practiced even a little bit of compassion training were nicer both to their loved ones and total strangers. And when you are kind, that kindness gets passed on. The world, even just your tiny little slice of it, is a better place.

Added bonus: You will get more writing done.

---

[*] This is just one study from 2011. Every year more research backs this up. See Susanne Leiberg, Olga Klimecki, and Tania Singer, "Short-Term Compassion Training Increases Prosocial Behavior in a Newly Developed Prosocial Game," *PLOS One* 6, no. 3 (March 2011), https://doi.org/10.1371/journal.pone.0017798.

## MEDITATION: LOVING-KINDNESS

To practice this kindness meditation, you will begin much as you have with the previous meditations. But instead of using a static anchor, you will repeat some specific phrases silently to yourself.

1.  Find a comfortable place to sit.
2.  Set a timer for five to fifteen minutes.
3.  Close your eyes if you wish. Take a few deep breaths. Now, instead of focusing your attention on an anchor, you're going to focus your attention on what are called *kindness phrases*.
4.  Repeat each phrase, silently in your mind, two or three times before moving on to the next.

> *May I be happy, truly happy.*
> *May I be healthy and strong.*
> *May I be safe and supported.*
> *May I be free from suffering.*
> *May I live a life of ease.*

Here I should warn you that sometimes these phrases can bring up unexpected emotions. You may notice that it feels selfish to wish yourself well, or you may wonder why you deserve a life of ease. Notice that. Get curious. Keep repeating the phrases and notice if your reactions to them change.

5.  Traditionally, the next step is to progress from focusing on the self to a loved one, to a neutral

person, then to a difficult person. For the record, there's nothing wrong with staying focused on yourself, especially if you feel you could use a little extra self-care, but if you'd like to try the full practice, simply bring to mind someone who is easy to care for, picture them in your mind, and change "I" to "you."

> *May you be happy, truly happy.*
> *May you be healthy and strong.*
> *May you be safe and supported.*
> *May you be free from suffering.*
> *May you live a life of ease.*

6. After repeating those phrases a few times, bring to mind a neutral person. This is generally someone you know by their title: the gardener, the checkout clerk at the grocery store, the receptionist. Picture them in your mind and repeat the phrases a few times.

7. Next, bring to mind someone who irks you. If there's no one in your life who fits the bill (lucky you), you can turn to politics and choose a public figure you disagree with. This part of the practice can be challenging. As you picture someone you dislike and wish them well, notice what comes up for you. Sometimes it can be helpful to picture them as a small child, or you can imagine what they would be like if they really were happy, healthy, safe, free from suffering, and living a life of ease.

8. Traditionally, in the Buddhist version of this meditation, we end by sending kind thoughts to all beings everywhere. I find it's a nice palate cleanser after the challenge of wishing a difficult person well.

*May all beings everywhere be happy, truly happy.*
*May all beings everywhere be healthy and strong.*
*May all beings everywhere be safe and supported.*
*May all beings everywhere be free from suffering.*
*May all beings everywhere live a life of ease.*

If this feels like a lot to remember, don't worry. You don't have to get the phrases exactly right. You can, and should, make them your own as you practice with them. You will come up with your own subtly different version over time. To start, you can use an abbreviated version and let one word resonate in your mind with each breath.

*Happy*
*Healthy*
*Safe*
*Free*
*Ease*

It's also helpful, when you're new to this practice, to use a recorded guided meditation. You can find one I created just for writers on the resources page for this book at SitWrite Here.com.

To get started, try doing this compassion practice once a week. Or if you find you like it, go ahead and use it every time you sit. As far as your writing is concerned, the loving-kindness phrases still work very well in terms of getting focused, because your mind will still wander, and you will still work to notice when it does so you can come back to the anchor; it's only that the anchor is now the kindness phrases.

## Diving Deeper into the Science of Kindness

To geek out on the science of kindness for a minute, on a physiological level, compassion practice serves to deactivate the sympathetic nervous system (SNS), the system in your body that responds to stress.

One of the body's quirks is that physiological stress responses don't discern between a memory of an event and something that is in fact happening. When you marinate in anger, fear, or sadness, the chemical signals in your body are the same as if you were actually experiencing the things that upset or scared you once upon a time. As we discussed in chapter 4, your brain registers and stores emotional discomfort even more so than physical suffering. When your SNS stays activated long after the event that triggered it, your body remains in a subtle but constant state of fight or flight.

Over time, the SNS becomes dominant and the functions of the parasympathetic nervous system (PNS), which works to calm you down, begin to shut down. This overstimulation of the SNS can lead to a system-wide imbalance. On a day-to-day basis, you may notice stomach trouble, anxiety, shallow breathing, an increased heart rate, poor quality of sleep, restlessness, night sweats, decreased libido, fatigue, nervousness, increased agitation/irritability, increased muscle tension, increased inflammation, increased susceptibility to infections, and more. This is a whole host of troubles that can be alleviated by simply allowing your sympathetic nervous system to rest.

When you see yourself in the world more clearly, you can acknowledge any stress that might be present in your life and, at the same time, bring conscious awareness to the fact that, in this moment, you are okay, even in the face of criticism and rejection.

## TAKING IT "OFF THE CUSHION"

Once you've been practicing meditation for a while, two things will happen in your day-to-day life (what meditators sometimes call "off the cushion"). First, as we've talked about in earlier chapters, you will start to notice the thoughts in your head. Second, you will become more discerning about which ideas, beliefs, and opinions are welcome to reside in your mind and which you would rather let go of.

Say you notice an internal monologue that sounds something like this: *I've been working on this book for years, I'm such a loser, who am I kidding trying to be a writer?* (It pains me to even write this—why are we so mean to ourselves?) This is precisely when you can choose kindness and try replacing that thought with the compassion phrases: *May I be happy. May I be healthy.*

If wishing good things for yourself seems like too big a

challenge, take heart. It's not something that comes easily to a lot of people. One thing you can try is simply amending the disparaging thought with some love. It might sound something like this: *I've been working on this book for years, I'm such a loser, but I choose to love myself anyway. May I be happy, truly happy. May I be healthy* . . . Noticing the thought and adding a healing intention is a good step. Before long you will notice the impulse to be mean to yourself, skip right over the harsh words, and land on: *May I be happy, truly happy.* You'll just be sending yourself love all day long. This is such a powerful practice. Kindness shifts the narrative and allows you to operate from a place of empowered action instead of shame and fear.

Try to remember this when things feel difficult. When your writing gets rejected, you may be tempted to launch into a downward spiral of doubt and self-loathing. The impulse is perfectly normal, don't worry, but remember where I started this book, with the story of how pain and suffering don't have to go together? With a little practice, you can begin to unwind the suffering so you don't get stuck in it.

## FEEL ALL THE FEELS

When you're in pain, it isn't useful to pretend you're not. Mindfulness is not about escaping from the world. It's about engaging with it fully, attempting to see things clearly as they truly are, in the present moment. Here I must take a moment to address what those of us in the mindfulness world call the *spiritual bypass.*

Spiritual bypass is when someone uses spiritual ideas or practices to avoid dealing with difficult emotions, unresolved trauma, or psychological wounds. Instead of doing the messy work of feeling grief, owning anger, and facing fear, they reach for comforting mantras, meditation, or "good vibes only" mindsets as a way to sidestep the discomfort. It might look like:

- Repeating "everything happens for a reason" instead of acknowledging someone's pain.
- Meditating to escape emotions rather than turn toward them.
- Using concepts like nonattachment to justify emotional detachment or disengagement.

If you get a rejection that hurts and decide you're way too mindful to suffer over it, so you take a deep breath, slap a smile on your face, and insist that you're fine when you're really not—that's a spiritual bypass. The danger of the spiritual bypass is that it looks like growth, but it's actually avoidance. Real spiritual practice doesn't skip over suffering. It helps us move through discomfort with honesty and compassion.

There's nothing wrong with you if you don't want to feel the pain of rejection. What's more, trauma (even little-t traumas like a rejection) can cloud your cognition and make it easy to slip into learned patterns of behavior from your childhood.

The troublesome reality is that, when you pretend something painful doesn't hurt, you create a significant mental burden for yourself. It takes energy to maintain an I'm-fine-everything's-fine smile. Letting yourself feel the sting of rejection fully may suck in the short term, but it will mean that, when you're ready, you can let it go and never have to deal with it again.

Let yourself feel the sadness because your story was rejected, the fear that your writing might not be good enough, the anxiety around what the hell you're even doing with your life. These are totally normal feelings.

If you open your inbox in the morning and find a rejection, it may be difficult to get any work done for a bit. Lean into it. If it was a minor blow, take a walk and just let yourself feel bad for an hour, then get back to work. If it was a biggie (a rejection for something you REALLY wanted and thought you had a good shot at), it might take longer.

I have been known to scoop a bowl of ice cream before noon and retreat to bed for the rest of the day. It's rare, but it happens. I've learned that giving myself the room to mourn allows me to wake up the next day feeling better and ready to get back to writing. If I don't give myself the space to feel what comes up, that sluggish, depressed feeling will follow me around for days, even weeks.

Believe it or not, big wins can be just as derailing. The day you open your email and find that you've won some big prize for your writing, you will very likely not get any writing done.

That's okay, too. Jump up and down, call your bestie, buy yourself some flowers, and enjoy all the fuzzy warm feelings. This, too, shall pass.

Mindfulness teaches us that there are no wrong feelings. You feel what you feel. Writers are often surprised to find that they aren't ecstatic when they finish their first draft. Sometimes it takes a while for the sense of accomplishment to set in, and that's okay. If you don't glow with excitement the moment you finish a draft, there's nothing wrong with you. Often, there are tears. If you've been working on a novel for a long time, you might even find yourself reluctant to finish. If you don't recognize that and address it, guess what? You'll never finish. Often these sorts of blocks can be difficult to recognize on your own, even with a regular practice of meditation. This is why community is so important.

## THE SANGHA

There are three pillars in traditional Buddhist teachings, usually referred to as the three jewels: the Buddha, the Dharma, and the Sangha.

The Buddha is of course the historical figure of Siddhartha Gautama, the mortal man who sat under a bodhi tree until he found enlightenment, but the word *buddha* is not a name. The translation of the word is roughly "one who is awake." As a core tenet of the teachings, it refers to the buddha inside each of us, the idea that we all have the capacity for deep wisdom and insight.

The Dharma is the collection of teachings that the Buddha

shared with the world, couched as invitations to explore your inner landscapes and find for yourself what is true.

Last (and most often ignored, especially in the West) is Sangha. Sangha is the community of practitioners who support and inspire one another in their journey. In the context of Buddhist teachings, community is held on the same level as the Buddha. It isn't just a nice thing to have, it's essential.

Remember my story from the "A Note from the Author" section about crying over onions and laughing all the while? I sometimes wonder, if I had been tasked with chopping those onions all by myself, would I have found such humor in the tears? I suspect not. Seeing my fellow veggie choppers wipe their eyes, hearing them sniff back tears, it all felt like a reflection of what I was going through. I felt solidarity in my discomfort, and that made all the difference.

The same holds true for writers. Engaging with other writers provides support through tough times, an exchange of ideas that can get you past blocks, and accountability—all things that you will need on your journey as a writer.

## Support Through the Tough Times

When you connect with other writers, you will find unique understanding and empathy. Your friends and loved ones may support you intellectually, but unless they have experienced the highs and lows, triumphs and setbacks, of the writing process, it will be difficult for them to truly understand what you're going through. Encouragement from your writing peers can provide the motivation needed to persevere in the face of self-doubt and rejection. Whether it's celebrating a published piece or offering a shoulder to cry on after a rejection, a supportive community reminds you that you are not alone in your creative endeavors.

## The Exchange of Ideas

One of the most significant benefits of being part of a writing community is how even a casual conversation can spark ideas. Talking with other writers, discussing style, structure, and character development, exposes you to different perspectives. It fosters growth and expands your horizons, encouraging you to try new things. What's more, when you find another writer (or writers) you click with, you can share your pages to get valuable feedback and constructive criticism that will help you take your writing to the next level.

## Accountability

Being part of a writing community keeps you motivated to do the work. Deadlines and commitments within the community can help you overcome procrastination and maintain a regular writing routine. The collective energy and shared dedication to the craft gently push you to achieve your writing goals by fostering productivity and personal growth.

And yet, even knowing all this, community often gets pushed aside as something that's nice to have if you can find it. Charming but optional. It's not. I strongly encourage you to reject the idea of the lone artist and find yourself a community of writers. It's so important.

## Isolation breeds self-doubt.
### –FABIENNE FREDRICKSON

For some, this might mean signing up for a class, attending a retreat, or joining a critique group. I've done all these things over the years, but I found they never lasted very long, and then I was right back to feeling lonely and isolated. Never was this more pronounced than in 2020, during the COVID lockdown. That was the year I decided to finally create the group I always wanted but could never find. I call it my *mindful writing community*.

We meet online every day of the week to meditate and write, plus we gather midweek for our community Q&A sessions. We discuss a lot of different things in the group, but we don't swap pages, and herein lies the beauty: There's no pressure to produce and it doesn't matter what you're writing. We have novelists, screenwriters, poets, journalists, and more. We just show up, meditate, do our writing, then hang out for a few minutes and support one another as writers, swapping stories, recommending books, and sharing opportunities. It has made a world of difference in my life and in my writing to have this wonderful community.

I strongly encourage you to find (or create) a community that works for you. It doesn't have to be the mindful writing community that I created (though you are absolutely welcome to come join us; check out my website for more information). You could share this book with a few writer friends and form a study group to test out which meditation practices work best for you, and then schedule regular meetings in person or online.

However you do it, set it as a top priority. Because here's the truth of it: As valuable as you know meditation is, as much as you know it will help you to write more and suffer less, actually doing it can be difficult. It's not your fault. Building any new practice into your routine takes time and discipline, and there are a number of studies that show how having social support can help you develop and sustain new habits.[*]

So, find a group. It might be the best thing you ever do for yourself as a writer.

◆

## PRACTICE & REFLECT

As you conclude your exploration of mindfulness and writing, use these practices to deepen your sense of balance, resilience, and connection to your writing community.

### LOVING-KINDNESS MEDITATION

Use this kindness practice to foster emotional resilience and kindness toward yourself and others. You can also visit SitWriteHere.com to download a guided loving-kindness meditation.

---

[*] In fact, a 2019 study showed specifically that incorporating social interaction into your writing routine can help inspire new ideas, improve focus, and increase productivity (among other benefits). See Meghan M. Bodenberg and Kristen Nichols, "Time for an 'Upgrade': How Incorporating Social Habits Can Further Boost Your Writing Potential," *Currents in Pharmacy Teaching and Learning* 11, no. 11 (November 2019): 1077–82, https://doi.org/10.1016/j.cptl.2019.07.003.

Instructions:

1. Set aside ten to fifteen minutes. Sit comfortably, close your eyes, and recite silently:

   *May I be happy, truly happy.*
   *May I be healthy and strong.*
   *May I be safe and supported.*
   *May I be free from suffering.*
   *May I live a life of ease.*

2. Gradually extend these phrases to others: loved ones, neutral people, difficult people, and finally all beings.

Reflection Questions:

• How did practicing loving-kindness affect your mood or mindset?
• Can you imagine how regular use of this practice might change your response to stress or rejection?

## NON-IDENTIFICATION PRACTICE

Practice distancing yourself from your thoughts, which will help you handle criticism or rejection more gracefully.

Instructions:

1. During your next writing session, notice the thoughts or feelings that arise, particularly any negative or self-critical ones.

2. Practice labeling these thoughts without ownership.
3. Instead of "I'm frustrated," say internally, "Frustration is present."
4. Instead of "My writing is terrible," note, "There is doubt."

REFLECTION QUESTIONS:

- How does reframing thoughts this way affect your emotional state?
- Can you see the potential to handle rejections differently using this method?

## EXPLORING YOUR MOTIVATION: WHY DO YOU WRITE?

Deepen your clarity about your writing motivations to help sustain persistence through challenges.

INSTRUCTIONS:

1. Write in a journal for fifteen minutes, answering this prompt: "I write because . . ."
2. Don't edit yourself. Just write freely and openly.

REFLECTION QUESTIONS:

- What surprised you about your answer?
- How might regularly revisiting your motivations support your writing practice?

## BUILDING YOUR WRITING SANGHA (COMMUNITY)

Reflect on the role of community in your writing life and make a concrete plan to deepen this connection.

Instructions:

1. Take ten minutes to brainstorm ways you might connect with other writers (join a class, find a critique partner, attend an event, or join an online community).
2. Pick one actionable step you can take this week toward building your community and write it down.

Reflection Questions:

- What barriers or hesitations come up when you think about reaching out?
- How can fostering community support your long-term writing goals?

# CONCLUSION

Writing is an act of courage. Every time you sit down to put words on the page, you're choosing vulnerability over comfort, creativity over certainty, connection over isolation. Those choices matter.

When you bring mindful awareness to your writing life, you learn to see yourself with honesty and compassion, to notice the thought patterns that support you and the ones that get in your way. You see your characters more distinctly, as full, complex beings shaped by their own inner worlds. You begin to see your work more honestly, not just the vision in your mind but what's actually there on the page. And most importantly, you come to see your relationship to that work with new understanding: Your writing matters, but it is not a measure of your worth.

When you write, you become part of an ongoing conversation about humanity. Every book, every poem, every scene you create adds to that conversation, rippling outward in ways you will never fully anticipate. No one else can say what you can. No one else carries your particular blend of experience, imagination, and heart.

The Buddhist teachings remind us that suffering eases when we understand our deep connection to one another. Writing is one of the ways we live that truth, shaping the world not through force but through empathy, imagination, and courage.

Sometimes clarity slips away. Doubt creeps in. Fear whispers that you're not enough. Life gets loud. So, I ask you to remember: The goal is not perfection, it's presence; not control, but clarity. *The world needs you to be brave.* It needs you to be messy and willing to show up.

Even when the words come slowly.

Even when no one seems to notice.

Even when the world feels too loud, too busy, too broken.

*Keep showing up.*

Because every sentence you craft is a stitch in the great tapestry of human understanding.

Every story you finish is a bridge to someone else's heart, built word by word, moment by moment.

And every time you sit down to write with clear eyes and an open heart, you are doing something sacred.

May you be happy.

May you be healthy.

May you be safe.

May you be free.

May you write more, and suffer less.

# APPENDIX: REASONS WE SOMETIMES AVOID OUR WRITING

've done a lot of thinking on "writer's block" over the years and worked with countless clients dealing with myriad forms of avoidance. In that time, I've devised a list of things that often masquerade as "writer's block":

1. The Inner Critic
2. Fear of What People Will Think
3. Burnout
4. Medical Challenges (for you or loved ones)
5. Distraction
6. Writing in the Wrong Format
7. Unrealistic Expectations
8. Material Is Too Fresh
9. Overwhelm
10. Not Knowing What Comes Next
11. The Story Isn't Yours Anymore

## #1: THE INNER CRITIC

We explored the inner critic extensively in chapter 3. Now I'd like to address the rest of the list. These tend to be a little easier to identify, which is to say they require less attunement to the subconscious, but the best way to recognize them is still to take a few minutes to meditate and ask yourself: "Why don't I feel like writing?"

If nothing comes to mind, scan through this list and see if anything jumps out at you. The important thing to remember is that there's always a reason why you're avoiding your writing, and once you can identify that reason you can address it, deal with it, and get back to work.

## #2: FEAR OF WHAT PEOPLE WILL THINK

It's far too easy to get caught up in worrying about what people will think about your writing. Particularly if you're writing about personal experience. People rarely sit down to write a memoir because their lives were perfect, and it's reasonable to be concerned about how your family/colleagues/community will feel about your story. It's also important to consider that revealing secrets through your writing could very likely damage relationships. That doesn't mean you shouldn't tell your story, just be sure you take the time to think about the possible fallout and whether the consequences are acceptable.

When the fear creeps in, notice the thoughts that arise and give them your attention. Sit with them. Decide what you're comfortable with and move forward with your story accordingly.

As for the opinions of other people, when you're writing nonfiction, you only have three options:

1.  **Get their blessing.** Tell the people in your life that you're writing a story in which they appear and offer to let them read it when you're done in the hopes of getting their blessing. You can offer to omit things they find objectionable or too personal. You don't have to. It's your story and as long as it's true, you're not required to get their stamp of approval. Which leads me to . . .

2.  **Get comfortable with the idea of blowback.** As long as you tell the story as truthfully as you can, you are legally free to do so. That said, you should definitely consult with a lawyer before publishing it, just to make sure you've done everything you can to protect yourself from legal action.

3.  **Wait 'em out.** You can always wait for the key players in your story to die before publishing. The timeline on this is shorter if the people you're writing about are older than you (parents or grandparents), but you can also wait until you yourself pass away and leave instructions for the story to be published after you're gone.

> If people wanted you to write warmly about them,
> they should have behaved better.
> —ANNE LAMOTT

If you're writing fiction and basing a character on a real person in your life, you might discover that your "writer's block" is rooted in the fear of how that individual might react to your portrayal of them. Recognize that anxiety and then you can take steps to address it. Change their names and alter a few key physical characteristics. If they're short in real life, make them tall in your story. Maybe turn your uncle into an aunt. Then practice saying, "It's fiction." You will probably be surprised how much people don't recognize themselves in your work.

If you're writing something that might shock your community (you're a schoolteacher writing erotica, for example), using a pen name can give you a comfortable layer of anonymity. Even if you're not trying to hide your identity but are taking a hard turn away from what you normally write and are worried that your readers will be disappointed, you can use a pen name for everything you write in your new genre.

If it's not so much about genre, but you're worried about what people will have to say about the topic you're tackling in your work, go ahead and open a fresh document and title it "Author's Note." Every time you feel like you need to explain yourself to your readers, open that file and do so.

In my second manuscript I had a section set in 1842, and I wanted my character to be reading a particular book that, thematically, fit the story perfectly. But in real life that book wasn't published until 1845. I was worried about people calling me out on that tiny detail. It seems silly now, but it felt paralyzing at the time. So I jumped to my "Author's Note" and wrote something along the lines of, "The astute reader might have noticed that the book Clara is carrying in chapter 18 hadn't yet been published in 1842 . . ." It helped calm the anxiety I had around anticipated criticism and enabled me to keep writing.

I ended up cutting that whole bit anyway.

## #3: BURNOUT

When I was writing my first novel, I was still working full-time and my kids were little. One Saturday, my husband took them to the park so I could have some quiet time to write. I got my coffee and settled in, but when I opened the document and looked at it, I experienced a sudden and overwhelming wave of nausea. I couldn't stand to even look at it.

I had been pushing so hard, waking up at 5 a.m. every day to write, and I was so tired. Frankly, the story felt like it was going nowhere and I just didn't have it in me to work on it that day. I was burned out.

Burnout tends to manifest in the body. If you notice that you don't want to write and find yourself feeling physically sluggish, exhausted, or even sick, you might be dealing with burnout. It can happen at any time with any project. The good news is that your story isn't doomed. Over the past many years, I've learned there are two main ways to deal with burnout.

1.  **Reconnect with the fun.** That day I got physically ill looking at my novel was the day I started working on my second novel. It was only an idea at that point, but I took the day to just play around with it, start an outline, do some research. Ever since then, I always like to have two novels going at any given time so I can take a break from one if I get sick of it, but for me, two is the limit. If I start a third project, I know I'm just avoiding finishing one of the other two. These numbers are specific to each writer. Some writers have five or six projects going at a time. Some can't fathom having more than one. If you fall into the one-project-at-a-

time camp, you really only have one option for how to deal with burnout: Take a break.

2. **Take a break.** Give yourself permission to step away from writing for a little while. The trick with taking a break is to decide how long the break will be, so it doesn't turn into quitting. Circle a date on your calendar and tell yourself, "Okay, on that day I will jump back into this project." Then put it out of your mind and allow yourself to not think about it. Go for long walks. Read books by other writers. Enjoy a midday nap. Take care of yourself, recharge, and when it's time, get back to work.

Either of these approaches will be more effective if you can layer in some support from fellow writers. We talked about this in chapter 6. Being in a community with other people allows us to stay grounded in Right View. When your mind wants to spin out and tell you you're a failure because you need a break, having other writers to balance that out and confirm that in fact rest is important, well, it just makes all the difference. Join writing groups or communities, or consider finding a mentor. Share your experiences and challenges with others who understand, who can provide valuable support and motivation.

Remember that burnout is common for writers. You are not alone. Be patient with yourself and give yourself the time and space you need to rediscover your love of writing.

## #4: MEDICAL CHALLENGES

Sometimes life throws you curveballs. Maybe it's a new diagnosis. Maybe it's a long-standing chronic illness. Maybe it's a loved one who is struggling. I would even include the first year with a new baby under this category. You may not appreciate it while you're in the midst of it, but that first year is tough—physically and emotionally. Babies can be such adorable little tyrants.

If you "don't feel like writing," take a moment to notice your thoughts, and realize it's because you're physically uncomfortable, haven't slept in three months, or you're distracted by caring for a loved one; there is no quick fix for that. There's no way around the fact that getting any writing done will be difficult.

If it's something temporary, a stomach bug or flu, just give yourself a pass and go back to bed. But if it's something ongoing, you will have to learn to work with it. My best advice is to be mindful of when impatience arises and do your best to take a deep breath and let it go. Remind yourself that you will have good days and bad days. Try to take some time on your good days to write, but keep the bar low.

People often laugh when I tell them that the foolproof way to always hit their goals is to make the goals easier, but sometimes, especially when you (or a loved one) aren't feeling well, making things easier is the best solution.

Maybe you only write 100 words a day, three days a week. You know what? That 100 words a day adds up.

## #5: DISTRACTION

There are all kinds of distractions. The first step in dealing with them is to get specific about what is distracting you. This will require a bit of mindful self-awareness to help you see your own habits clearly.

Is it your phone that is yanking your attention? Is it all the other things you "should be doing"? Is it social media? For these types of distractions, the best solution is to set a timer. I suggest investing a few dollars in a kitchen timer (so that you can leave your phone in the other room). First, set it for ten minutes and meditate. Then, set it for one hour and write. There is almost nothing that can't wait seventy minutes.

For me, when the kids were little, the mere fact that they were conscious and moving about was distracting. As soon as they were awake, a little part of my brain would start listening for fights, tracking their movements around the house, and being wary of too much quiet—a sure indication that someone was doing something they shouldn't. I couldn't seem to shut it off, but once I recognized it, I could structure my days around it instead of trying to fight it.

If you find yourself facing distractions that can't be put on hold for seventy minutes, the solution here is twofold.

1. **Get up early or stay up late.** Make an hour for yourself in the part of the day when nothing is expected of you. I have come to truly love the early hours of the morning, when the kids are safe in their beds and everything is quiet. Getting up early or staying up late is also a good solution if you have a day job that asks a lot of you. Hopefully, no one is expecting you to respond to Slack messages at 5 a.m. or 9 p.m. If they are, you might need to step back and consider setting some stronger boundaries. Use the time outside work to do your creative writing.

2. **Think about what work you can do while you are distracted.** There's a lot of what I call "writing-adjacent" work that goes into being a writer. I still struggle to write a first draft without quiet, but I can write a blog post, or make a list of publications to send a short story to, or respond to an email from my agent while sitting in a plastic chair at my boy's tae kwon do dojang, which (seriously) might be the loudest place on earth. Learn what tasks you can do despite distractions and make the most of the noisy times.

## #6: WRONG FORMAT

One of the reasons people get stuck is that they're trying to force a story into the wrong format. For whatever reason, they're not seeing their own work clearly. Maybe they think they're writing a short story when really it needs to be a novel. Maybe they think it's a poem when it's actually a memoir. Maybe that novel is actually an essay.

In 2023, I had an idea for a new novel. I had written about 10,000 words in fits and starts, and I wanted some focused time to dive in and figure it out. So, I took myself on a writing retreat, excited to make some real progress on it.

The week started off well. I wrote roughly 13,000 words in the first two days, exploring characters and drafting scenes that had been percolating in my head, but on the third day everything slowed down. I simply couldn't think of what else to write. I began to worry. *What if writer's block really IS a thing?* Not only was it a concern for my immediate circumstances but I would have had to write a letter of apology to every writer I'd ever worked with.

I pulled out this list (the one you're reading through right now) to coach myself and paused here at "Wrong Format." As soon as I saw the words, I knew that was it. I was writing a novella. I had always suspected the project would be short (it's political satire), but realizing it was a novella suddenly made the whole structure fall into place.

I googled the word count range for novellas (it's 10,000–40,000) and was flooded with a mix of relief and excitement. I never intended to write a novella. I mean, who even publishes novellas? Not my problem. I'd rather write a satisfying little novella that never sees the light of day than spend years trying to force it to be a novel.

I spent Thursday and Friday reorganizing what I had into a new structure, writing some scenes that suddenly needed to be written (no more "writer's block" here), and then BAM, I had a first draft. Oh, the satisfaction!

If you're feeling blocked and think you might be writing in the wrong format, take this handy little quiz:

1. Why did you choose the current format for your story? That is, if you think you're writing a novel, ask yourself: Why a novel?
   - It's what I've always written (give yourself one point).
   - The story I'm telling is well suited to this format (zero points).
2. Have you considered other formats (poetry, essay, memoir, novella—even if you've never written them before)?
   - It never occurred to me (one point).
   - Yes, I'm format-fluid (zero points).
3. Are you currently reading a lot in the format you're trying to write (for example: You are trying to write a novel and are reading a lot of novels)?
   - No (one point).
   - Yes (zero points).

If you scored any points at all, you might be writing in the wrong format. If so, the invitation is to notice if you have a gut response to being "wrong." I've seen many writers try to force a story to be something it's not because, for whatever reason, they have an intense aversion to accepting that the framework might be something different from what they initially devised. If you find yourself in this position, take heart. This is one of those rare times in life when realizing you've been wrong can actually be really exciting.

Give yourself permission to explore other styles of storytelling, to grow and change as a writer. Consider the possibilities that could await you as you embrace a new style of storytelling.

## #7: UNREALISTIC EXPECTATIONS

Writers have healthy imaginations. It's kind of our thing. But your imagination can work against you when you get caught up in expectations. Rigid expectations can create a paralyzing sense of pressure and anxiety, both of which frequently masquerade as "writer's block." I have found this to be true on the grand scale as well as in smaller, more nuanced ways.

First, the grand. It's perfectly normal to imagine your enormous royalty checks, your NPR interviews and TED Talks, the fame that will inevitably come once your book is published, but dreaming of having written a successful book is TOTALLY different from writing it. Don't let expectations of wealth and fame distract you from the writing itself.

To be clear, there's nothing wrong with fantasizing about success. It's healthy to have a vision for what you want, but you also have to be willing to put your butt in the chair and write on a regular basis. Writing a book takes work. Writing a wildly successful book takes a lot of work and a fair amount of luck, and since you can't really control the luck part, all you can do is get writing.

Second, the more nuanced. Even when you keep your big expectations in check, you can still get tripped up by what you expect to accomplish on any given day.

If you sit down to write expecting to put 1,000 words on the page, but only get 100, you might find yourself discouraged. If it happens a lot, you might even think about giving up, but keep in mind that writing is a long game. Sometimes you will need to do things that don't even look like writing, such as taking a long walk, or reading someone else's work. It's all part of the job.

The solution is to ask yourself why you set that expectation for yourself in the first place. If your goal was to write 1,000 words, it was probably because you're trying to make progress on your draft. In that case, 100 words is still progress. Pat yourself on the back and keep going.

When I was halfway through writing this book, I got distracted. The holiday season rolled around and my coaching business was having a busy period. I had to cancel some of my scheduled writing times to make room for other commitments. Around mid-December I realized it had been two weeks since I had written anything, but there wasn't much I could do about it at the time. Life was just really busy. It was unrealistic to think I could do everything.

Instead of beating myself up for not writing (shooting myself with that second arrow), I scrolled forward a few weeks in my calendar to January and blocked out time to write. My plan was to work on the manuscript for twelve hours a week.

But when the first week of January rolled around, things kept coming up that needed my attention. There was a lot happening with my family: important doctor appointments, school visits, helping my mom move. Family is the one thing that almost always takes priority over my writing. Every time, I asked myself, "Is this more important than my writing?" When the answer was yes, I had to cancel my writing time and do the thing that was more important, so that first week of January, I didn't get any writing done.

At the end of the week, I reset. Week two would be different, I said. But then our family was evacuated in the middle of the night to escape the Eaton Fire that was consuming the neighborhood of Los Angeles County immediately to the east of us. It took two weeks to get back home, to have our power restored, and to reconnect with any semblance of normalcy.

And I reset again. By the last week of January, I was able to eke out three hours of writing, and it was a rough three hours. I had to review the manuscript and remember my intentions for the different chapters. I got tired easily.

But I kept my goal in mind, reset again, and managed to hit five hours the following week. The week after that, it bumped up to seven. It was March before I finally had a week where I wrote for a full twelve hours. Three months. It took me three months to get back into a regular writing routine.

I share this here to give you an honest perspective on the fact that making time for your writing can be hard. Be gentle with yourself and hold your expectations loosely. Ask yourself why you have the expectations you have. There have been plenty of times in my life when writing three hours a week was plenty, but right now, as I write this, I also have two half-finished novels I want to get back to, a new story idea I can't wait to dive into, and a romance series I've outlined, just for fun. That's at least six books I want to write (or have already partially written), and I can't work on any of them until I finish this one, so right now I really want to be writing as much as I can.

The danger in sharing specific numbers, I realize, is that you will compare your writing practice to mine and judge yourself, or me, lacking. My hope is that my sharing will guide you to some reasonable expectations and help you to keep in mind that writing takes time to build up into a regular routine. The pressure of expectations almost always comes from comparing yourself to others. Try to recognize the trap of comparison as the pointless game it is and set expectations that are right for you. Do this by meditating on the regular so you can notice the thoughts that cross your mind and discern between the ones that are useful and the ones that aren't.

Instead of aiming for perfection, focus on making progress. Give yourself permission to make mistakes. And most importantly, just keep writing.

## #8: THE MATERIAL IS TOO FRESH

This challenge surfaces most commonly for writers working on personal essays or memoir, but it can apply to fiction, poetry, and screenplays, too.

If you're working on a fiction project, working with material that is too fresh simply means you need to do more research. Dig deep into the emotional lives of your characters (we talk about this more in chapter 4), research the setting, explore what is happening in their world. If you're writing historical fiction, this could mean you need to research the geopolitical conditions of your characters' lives. If you're writing fantasy, you may need to do more world-building. For poetry, you may need to better understand what inspired the piece before you can finish it. This is legitimate writing time and, frankly, a lot of fun. Do your research. Contact experts. Dive headfirst into internet rabbit holes. Enjoy! As you answer questions about your work, it will naturally start to take shape.

Things get a little trickier with nonfiction. Writing about how you've overcome something difficult or traumatic is a beautiful act of generosity. Sharing your story allows others to know they are not alone and can be a great source of strength for anyone struggling with what you have already been through, but in writing about your personal experiences, there are a couple of ways that tackling fresh material can be paralyzing.

1.  **Lack of perspective.** When an idea or experience is still fresh in your mind, the emotional intensity of it can prevent you from finding the objectivity needed to explore it fully. Writing a story requires some reflection and analysis, which can be hindered if you are too close to the subject matter.

2.  **Pressure to capture everything.** When an experience is fresh, there is often a subconscious desire to capture every detail accurately and vividly in your writing. This pressure to do justice to the experience can result in performance anxiety that inhibits your creative flow. You may feel compelled to find the perfect words or phrases, which can lead to self-censorship and a debilitating fear of making mistakes.

When you're writing about something that happened in real life, you first need to create a little bit of distance between yourself and the material. Start by journaling (and by that I mean freewriting, using a pen and paper). It's an excellent way to begin the processing that needs to take place in your brain before you can think about creating a story for public consumption.

> Make sure you're sharing from your scars,
> not your open wounds.
> —GLENNON DOYLE

A 2022 meta-analysis of thirty-one experiments found that expressive writing (writing about your thoughts and feelings) helped to reduce symptoms of depression, anxiety, and stress. It's worth noting that the benefits aren't immediate.* It takes some time to see the benefits of journaling. How long is different for everyone, but the study shows that benefits increased with the frequency of the journaling. Those who wrote in their journals every one to three days experienced the most benefit. Talk therapy and eye movement desensitization and reprocessing (EMDR) are wonderful complements to this practice.

The important thing to keep in mind is that the first time you talk about, touch into, or write through something big that happened to you, it will not be ready to share publicly. Give yourself permission to process. Once you feel you have some perspective, come back to it with the intention of creating something for other people to read and know that, even then, it will be a first draft. Be patient with yourself and just keep writing.

## #9: OVERWHELM

The task of writing a whole book can be overwhelming. The limitless possibilities of storytelling, combined with the seem-

---

* For more information, see Lin Guo, "The Delayed, Durable Effect of Expressive Writing on Depression, Anxiety and Stress: A Meta-Analytic Review of Studies with Long-Term Follow-Ups," *British Journal of Clinical Psychology* 62, no. 1 (March 2023): 272–97, https://doi.org/10.1111/bjc.12408.

ingly insurmountable task of transforming thoughts into words, can create a solid brick wall between you and your dream of a finished book. The more writers delve into the world of literature, the more they may feel a sense of insignificance or a daunting realization of how much they have still to learn and achieve.

Anytime a specific task (like writing) feels overwhelming, notice that and ask yourself if there's a way to break it into smaller pieces. There are no rules for writing. Your job as a writer is to mindfully find what works for you.

My advice: Never (ever) sit down to try and write a book. Don't even sit down to try to write a short essay. Instead, sit down and try to write 500 words. This can help you to find a more manageable whelm. Know that finishing a project will take time, and that's a good thing. You can continue to learn and hone your craft along the way. You don't have to know everything, and you don't need to worry about themes, character arcs, or structure when you're writing your first draft. There will be plenty of opportunity for the nuances of storytelling once you get rolling with your project.

If you are an outliner, which is to say that you like to know where you're going before you start, go ahead and outline, but don't let anyone tell you it's required. Try outlining. If it works for you, great. If not, no biggie. For me it's different for every project.

I didn't outline my first novel, and it took me about eight years to figure out the story. Before I started my second novel, I had been playing around with the outline for a while. It was almost fifty pages long. I had thought out every beat. That story was a breeze to write and I swore I would never write another book without outlining, but then a friend proposed that we do NaNoWriMo one year, and I eagerly hopped into writing a new story with only an inkling of what it was even about.* #Noregrets

While we're on the topic of where you should start, let me also say you don't need to write your introduction, first chapter, or opening line first. In fact, it's tremendously difficult to write the first bit first. You will learn so much over the course of writing your project. Trying to consider everything from page one is a sure way to overwhelm yourself, and you will almost certainly have to come back and completely rewrite your opening anyway, so don't torture yourself.

## #10: NOT KNOWING WHAT COMES NEXT

In the labyrinth of creativity, every writer, at some point, finds themselves at a crossroads, staring down the branching path ahead, not sure which way to go. Take heart, this is totally normal.

There are a few things you can try to get yourself out of this predicament.

- Meditate. Stress impedes creativity, so simply taking the time to focus on your breath and stop ruminating on the fact that you're stuck can help unstick you and make some space for creative solutions to rise into consciousness.

---

* National Novel Writing Month (NaNoWriMo) is an annual writing challenge where writers all over the world try to write 50,000 words in the month of November. It can be a fun way to make serious progress on a first draft.

- Take a walk without your phone. Bring a notebook and pen instead. Look around you. Soak up your surroundings and just be open to whatever thoughts arise. You don't have to specifically think about your story. Let the question of what happens next just rest. Often you find what you're looking for when you stop looking.

- Dive a little deeper into what your characters want. We talk about this more in chapter 4, but still, know that your characters' motivations are what will move your story forward. Grab a notebook or some scratch paper and spend some time freewriting about what they're after.

- Make a list of fifty things that could happen. Don't stop at ten or twenty. Get all the way to fifty. Get past the rational ideas and have some fun with this. You will almost certainly be surprised by what you come up with.

- Read in your genre. Sometimes just reading someone else's work will spark ideas. Please note that I'm not suggesting that you copy another person's story. I am encouraging you to be open to how other stories can spark ideas for you.

- Read outside your genre. Often the answers to your questions aren't rooted in a specific genre or a list of curated titles designed to unlock the mind's hidden chambers. Instead, it is the transformative act of reading itself that offers new avenues of exploration. It doesn't matter what you read; the key is to just keep reading.

- Ask AI. If you haven't yet tried working with a large language model (LLM) like ChatGPT or Claude, I strongly encourage you to give it a try. Explain to it what you're writing, tell it where you're stuck, and hit ENTER.

It will toss some suggestions your way that just might get your creative juices flowing.*

It may be the case that you know what you're seeking, even if you can't yet articulate it. The very act of letting go of a specific goal allows the subconscious the freedom to explore, to play, and to find what you didn't even know you were looking for, drawing parallels and generating insights from the most unexpected sources, but it doesn't work well when you're caught up in stressful thoughts about the past or future.

So, take a breath. Take a walk. Take a shower or a nap. Stop looking, and there's a pretty good chance you'll find the answers.

## #11: THE STORY ISN'T YOURS ANYMORE

Once upon a time, my husband and I were out on a date, and we started thinking about what our younger selves would think about our relationship. What if, after our first kiss, we had been shown a short clip of our lives fifteen years later, with two little kids and demanding jobs. What would we have thought? Then we had a little fun with the idea: "What if two young people, madly in love, leaned in for their first kiss, and as they pulled away, they found that ten years had gone by and they were getting divorced?" We liked the idea

---

* A lot of writers are uncomfortable with AI technology, but it's just a tool. What's more, it's not going away, so pretending it doesn't exist is foolish. You don't have to use it, but understanding it, at least a little, puts the power back in your hands.

of them trying to figure out how they had gone from that glowing blush of infatuation to screaming about who gets to keep the cat.

I loved this idea. I jotted it down as soon as we got home, and it sat on the side of my desk for months. Then, at some point, it got filed into my story idea file because I didn't have time to work on it, but I always intended to. I always wanted to come back and write an outline for the novel.

A few years went by and I heard that Liane Moriarty had published a new book about a woman who slips and hits her head and forgets the previous ten years of her life. She thinks she's in love and engaged to be married, but finds that in fact she's a bossy mother of three going through a divorce. It was the same idea.

Am I saying that Liane Moriarty stole my story? Absolutely not. That story was looking for someone who would tell it. It landed on me for a night, but when I wouldn't give it the time or energy it needed to become a book, it hopped along and found someone who would take it seriously.

I know this sounds crazy, but I share it because sometimes, when you have an idea for a story but you ignore it for a while and then try to come back to it, there's just no juice left in it. The passion is gone. You know it's a good idea, but you just don't get excited when you think about working on it. That's when you know it's not your story anymore.

Sadly, the only solution is to let it go. This can be hard, especially if it was an idea that you were initially super excited about, but take heart. The fact that you had that idea means that you have been doing the work of nurturing your creativity. More ideas will come.

When they do, you'll want to take care with how much,

and when, you choose to talk about them, because another way to lose a story is by talking too much about it too soon. When you're working out the details of a story, it's highly susceptible to criticism. What's more, because you're still figuring it out, you're probably not great at telling it yet. It may be a fantastic story, but when you do a piss-poor job of explaining it to a friend and they respond with "meh" it can really dampen your enthusiasm for it.

So when is it safe to talk about a project? It's different for everyone. Some writers can talk about a story at any time throughout the process. Others won't breathe a peep until the book has been sent off to the publisher.

For me, it's about getting through the first draft. Before I'm done with the first draft, I'll just say, "I'm working on a new idea." That's literally all I can say, or else a discussion opens up, and before I know it, the idea just wilts. I can almost feel it happen. It starts as a little knot of anxiety when someone asks what I'm writing, and as I talk the sensation expands. This is when I have to say, "I can't talk about it yet. I'm still figuring it out." If I don't, if I talk too long, there's a point at which I feel a sudden deflation, and I know I won't be able to work on it again. It's gone.

But once I have a first draft down, it seems I can discuss the story all I want. I'll share the basic premise with friends to get their thoughts, to see what questions they ask. Those questions often fuel my revisions as I start to understand what perspectives different people will bring to the premise.

So pay attention to how you feel when you talk about your work. Even if you don't understand what you feel or can't explain it, respect it.

# MEDITATION INDEX

This section is designed as a reference, a place you can return to when you want to quickly find one of the meditations introduced throughout the book. Each practice is listed here in its simplest form, along with a brief note to remind you of its purpose and how to use it.

That said, the meditations don't live in isolation. You'll get the deepest benefit if you explore them first in their full context, where you can see how each practice connects to the challenges and joys of the writing life. Think of this section not as a replacement for those chapters but as a companion you can flip to whenever you need a nudge back to the cushion, or to the page.

Also, keep in mind that I've created a collection of free guided meditations, one for each practice in this section. You can find them on my website at SitWriteHere.com, and use them as companions to deepen your practice whenever you like.

**Chapter 1 Meditation**

## BASIC INSIGHT MEDITATION AND WRITING

This practice is an entry point into mindfulness: simple, grounding, and endlessly adaptable. By beginning with the breath (or another anchor) and gently returning whenever the mind wanders, you train yourself in the art of noticing, a skill that translates beautifully to the page.

Practically, this meditation starts with ten minutes of focused awareness, followed by a seamless shift into an hour of writing. The trick is to carry the same observational stance from meditation into your work. Thoughts will arise, and when you notice them, you get to choose whether to follow them or let them go.

INSTRUCTIONS:

1. Set a timer for ten minutes.
2. Get comfortable. Sit in a chair with your feet on the floor or on a cushion with your legs crossed. Let your hands rest gently in your lap.
3. Choose an anchor. Focus on your breath, the sounds in the room, or even a mental countdown from ten to zero.
4. Observe without judgment. When your mind wanders (because it will), simply notice the thought, acknowledge it, and gently return to your anchor.
5. When the timer goes off, consider that you're not ending the meditation so much as shifting the anchor.

Instead of focusing on your breath, or the sounds in the room, you will focus on your writing. Thoughts will still arise; you're simply going to notice them. If they're useful, follow them; if not, let them go and keep writing.

6. Do this for one hour.

**Chapter 2 Meditation**

## STILLNESS PRACTICE

This meditation invites you to explore the power of simply being, of resting in stillness with presence and patience. By holding still, you come face-to-face with the subtle impulses of the body and mind, and learn to soften into discomfort with curiosity.

The practice begins much like basic insight meditation: You choose an anchor, settle, and breathe. The difference is that you add the commitment to remain as still as possible, noticing the urge to move and choosing awareness over reaction.

1. Begin by finding a comfortable place to sit.
2. Set a timer for five to fifteen minutes.
3. Close your eyes if you wish, and allow yourself to settle, take a few deep breaths. Connect with your body, feel its weight and presence. Choose an anchor for your attention, such as your breath, a sensation in your body, or the ambient sounds around you. This anchor will serve as your point of return, a steady base to which you can come back whenever your mind begins to wander. So far this is precisely what you've been practicing already in this book.

4. Now you add a deliberate practice of stillness. Once you've begun, try to remain as still as possible, resisting the urge to scratch an itch, adjust your posture, or engage in any other movement.* Sounds easy enough, right? It's actually quite challenging.

Maintain the stillness for the duration of the meditation or until the discomfort edges into pain.

**Chapter 3 Meditation**

## EXPLORING AVERSION

Every writer meets resistance from time to time, those moments when the page feels impossible to face. This practice helps you turn toward that resistance with honesty and compassion, so you can understand what's really getting in the way instead of relinquishing your power to "writer's block."

Begin with a few minutes of insight meditation, then gently inquire into why you're avoiding the work. By noticing the cause (whether it's noise, uncertainty, self-doubt, or something else), you can choose a constructive next step, reclaim your focus, and return to the page with clarity.

1. Set your timer and sit in a comfortable position.
2. Choose an anchor to rest your attention on, a place to

---

* Unless you are an advanced meditator, I suggest that you don't try to refrain from the involuntary subtle movements that come with breathing and swallowing. Let your body be comfortable.

bring your mind back to when it wanders (because it will).

3. After about five minutes, turn your attention toward the question of why you're avoiding your work and just notice what thoughts come up. What you will inevitably discover is that there's always a reason that you don't feel like writing.

   - Maybe your children are being noisy and you need quiet.
   - Perhaps you don't know how to start your story.
   - It could be that you're feeling discouraged or unsure of yourself.

4. Once you know what that reason is, you can assess it and, instead of just succumbing to "writer's block," decide how to *act*.

   - Send the kids to the park for an hour.
   - Jump in at your second chapter and come back to write the first one later.
   - Read a book on craft, or take a course.

As soon as you have the answer you need, you can either end the meditation or continue to sit until the bell rings, because, hey, you're already meditating, why not finish it out?

## Chapter 5 Meditation

Chapter 5 includes two meditations that work together to help you access and explore your emotions. The first guides you in intentionally evoking a specific feeling, while the second teaches you how to notice emotions as they naturally arise in the body.

## EVOKING SPECIFIC EMOTIONS

Writing comes alive when emotions pulse on the page, and this meditation helps you tap directly into that well. By recalling a moment when you felt a strong emotion, you practice staying present with it long enough to understand how it moves through you.

Spend the first ten minutes in simple insight meditation, then invite in a memory tied to the emotion you want to explore. Notice the physical sensations it stirs, then capture those details in writing, giving your characters and scenes a deeper authenticity.

1. Set your timer for fifteen minutes.
2. For the first ten minutes, simply focus on your anchor.
3. Then, intentionally bring to mind a time when you felt the emotion you wish to explore. Really revel in the memory and notice how it feels in your body. It will likely be unpleasant, but just see how long you can be with it.

As soon as the timer goes off (or you feel like you've had enough), take a deep breath, then end the meditation.

Write down everything you can recall about the physical sensations associated with that emotion. Don't worry about overwriting. You can always edit later.

## NOTICING YOUR OWN EMOTIONS

This meditation invites you to turn inward with kindness and patience, meeting your emotions as they arise in the body. It's a gentle but powerful way to become familiar with your own emotional landscape, one sensation at a time.

Begin with a foundation of insight meditation before scanning the body for subtle sensations (tightness, warmth, or tingling) that may carry emotional tones. By naming and exploring what you discover, then writing it down, you practice the art of translating felt experience into words, a skill that deepens both presence and prose. Because this practice includes two parts (cultivating open awareness followed by exploration), it takes more time. I recommend starting with twenty-five minutes.

1. The first step is to identify emotional sensations. Start with the basic Insight Meditation described in chapter 1, noticing thoughts that arise, letting them go, and coming back to the anchor. After about ten minutes (it can be helpful to set a timer), turn your attention inward and scan your body for any pronounced physical sensations, usually in the front of the torso, neck, throat, or face. It can take a while to notice these sensations, so be patient. Eventually, you might notice tightness, or warmth, or tingling. When you notice something, get curious. Is there an emotional component to it? There might be. Or there might not. You might notice your stomach rumbling and realize you're hungry. That's fine. But if you turn your attention to a tightness in

your chest and suddenly notice sadness arising, you have tapped into some stored emotions.

2. The next step is to explore. When you notice a specific emotion, and if you feel steady, turn your attention toward it. Investigate with curiosity. You might label it with whatever word comes to mind. For instance: sadness. Then try to stay with it for a few seconds and check in again. Does it still feel like sadness or has it shifted into something else? Get curious about it and ask yourself, "What is sadness? What does it feel like?" With no stories built up around it, just in this moment, right now, what are you experiencing?

3. When you feel like you've explored the emotion even a little bit, try to write down what you've experienced. The point of this exercise is twofold: You're learning to explore emotions from a strong, steady base, then practicing the art of putting words to those feelings.

4. Sometimes the experience of somatic emotions will not be as clear-cut as what I described. Perhaps you notice a sensation in your neck or jaw, but it doesn't seem to be connected to anything in particular. It doesn't "feel" like any specific emotion. In that case, just label the actual sensation: tightness, warmth, or even "something." If it's unpleasant, you can label it that: "unpleasant." Then, again, get curious. Does it change as you bring your attention to it? "More unpleasant" or "less unpleasant" or maybe "tightness" may turn to "aching." Try to be present with it, as it is, moment to moment, using your writerly skills to label it as specifically as possible. Sit with it for as long as is comfortable (or maybe even a little uncomfortable), then come back to your anchor.

You can also put a hand on your heart, or open your eyes to ground yourself back in the here and now.

Remember to be kind with yourself and go slowly. This can be tricky work.

## Chapter 6 Meditation

## INVITE YOUR INNER CRITIC TO THE WORK

Rather than banishing your inner critic, this practice invites them to take a seat at the table as an ally. With mindfulness as your foundation, you can learn to hear that voice not as a saboteur but as a discerning partner in revision.

Begin with a short meditation to steady your awareness before turning to your draft. From there, read with curiosity, letting your inner critic raise questions about clarity, consistency, and emotional resonance. Always steer the critique toward "Is it working?" rather than "This is terrible."

1. Find a comfortable place to sit.
2. Set a timer for five to fifteen minutes.
3. Close your eyes if you wish. Take a few deep breaths. Choose an anchor for your attention, a place to come back to when the mind wanders.
4. When the bell rings, open your eyes and read your work. Pay close attention to questions such as:
    - Do the physical descriptions show the reader what you're picturing in your mind?
    - Is this character behaving in a way that aligns with what you know about them?

- Do the emotions in each scene unfold as a natural progression of everything that has come before?
- Do you notice any physical responses in your body as you read through sections that were meant to be emotional?

Embrace this opportunity for your inner critic to shine. Just remember that engaging your inner critic while editing doesn't mean succumbing to negativity or self-doubt. Instead, adopt a mindset of constructive criticism, where the goal is to challenge your work to be its best version. Listen to that critical inner voice, but maintain confidence in your creative vision. If you find your inner critic is getting the upper hand, try to take a half step sideways into discernment. Instead of telling yourself "This is terrible," try asking "Is it working?"

**Chapter 7 Meditation**

## LOVING-KINDNESS

This meditation softens the edges of self-criticism and reconnects you to compassion for yourself, for others, and for the wider world. It's an antidote to the harshness that can creep into the writing process, reminding you that creativity flourishes best in a spirit of care.

Practically, you repeat simple kindness phrases in your mind, first for yourself, and then (if you wish) extending them outward to loved ones, neutral people, and even those you struggle with. By cultivating this mindset before or after writing, you create a gentler, more generous relationship with your work and the people it may one day reach.

1.  Find a comfortable place to sit.
2.  Set a timer for five to fifteen minutes.
3.  Close your eyes if you wish. Take a few deep breaths. Now, instead of focusing your attention on an anchor, you're going to focus your attention on what are called *kindness phrases.*
4.  Repeat each phrase, silently in your mind, two or three times before moving on to the next.

> *May I be happy, truly happy.*
> *May I be healthy and strong.*
> *May I be safe and supported.*
> *May I be free from suffering.*
> *May I live a life of ease.*

Here I should warn you that sometimes these phrases can bring up unexpected emotions. You may notice that it feels selfish to wish yourself well, or you may wonder why you deserve a life of ease. Notice that. Get curious. Keep repeating the phrases and notice if your reactions to them change.

1.  Traditionally, the next step is to progress from focusing on the self to a loved one, to a neutral person, then to a difficult person. For the record, there's nothing wrong with staying focused on yourself, especially if you feel you could use a little extra self-care, but if you'd like to try the full practice, simply bring to mind someone who is easy to care for, picture them in your mind, and change "I" to "you."

*May you be happy, truly happy.*
*May you be healthy and strong.*
*May you be safe and supported.*
*May you be free from suffering.*
*May you live a life of ease.*

2. After repeating those phrases a few times, you bring to mind a neutral person. This is generally someone you know by their title: the gardener, the checkout clerk at the grocery store, the receptionist. Picture them in your mind and repeat the phrases a few times.

3. Next, bring to mind someone who irks you. If there's no one in your life who fits the bill (lucky you), you can turn toward politics and choose a public figure you disagree with. This part of the practice can be challenging. As you picture someone you dislike and wish them well, notice what comes up for you. Sometimes it can be helpful to picture them as a small child, or you can imagine what they would be like if they really were happy, healthy, safe, free from suffering, and living a life of ease.

4. Traditionally, in the Buddhist version of this meditation, we end by sending kind thoughts to all beings everywhere. I find it's a nice palate cleanser after the challenge of wishing a difficult person well.

*May all beings everywhere be happy, truly happy.*
*May all beings everywhere be healthy and strong.*
*May all beings everywhere be safe and supported.*
*May all beings everywhere be free from suffering.*
*May all beings everywhere live a life of ease.*

If this feels like a lot to remember, don't worry. You don't have to get the phrases exactly right. You can, and should, make them your own as you practice with them. You will come up with your own subtly different version over time. To start, you can use an abbreviated version and let one word resonate in your mind with each breath.

*Happy*
*Healthy*
*Safe*
*Free*
*Ease*

The exact words matter less than the spirit behind them. What's most important is the willingness to return, again and again, to a place of kindness, especially when it feels hardest. Over time, this gentle discipline can transform not only your writing but also the way you relate to yourself and others.

# ACKNOWLEDGMENTS

Thank you to my agent, Lisa Hagan; my editor, Joel Fotinos; and the entire team at St. Martin's Essentials (especially Emily Anderson—go Vikings!).

To the writers in the Mindful Writing Community, including Caroline Grant, Kimberly Glassman, Lori Oliwenstein, Katie Clary, Kathy Fleig, Laura Ax-Fultz, Linda Watkins, Nancy Wallis, Natalie Sayth, Stacey Bennetts, Derek Surka, Margaret Ranger, Jenny Devlin, Nancy D'Aurizio, Wanda Chui, Kathleen Anderson, and Cyndera Quackenbush: Thank you! You have been with me every step of the way, and I'm so grateful for all of you. Thank you, thank you, thank you for being with me on this journey.

A big thank-you to the other early supporters of the book: Carolyn West, Candace Coakley, Don Pierson, Doug Grant, Dr. Bob Newport, Elena M. Rodriguez, Heather Renee, Kathy Burdette, Lana Diamond Weinstein, Laurie Anderson, LaTeigra Cahill, Leslie Rodd, Mayer Martin, Melissa J. Spencer, Mike and Emily Aerni, Rachel Eddowes, and Sherry Mossafer Rind.

Thank you to my team at Sit Write Here, especially Joy

Santos and John Soriano. Without your help, I wouldn't have any time to write. I'm so grateful for all the ways you support me, our clients, and our community as a whole. And to Crystal Adaway, for her thoughtful feedback on this project specifically.

Deep gratitude to my mindfulness teachers, including Tara Brach, Mark Coleman, Howard Cohen, Oren Jay Sofer, Jessica Morey, Cara Lai, Spring Washam, Celeste Young, George Hass, and especially to Jack Kornfield, who taught the first daylong I ever sat and has been my guide on this journey for over two decades.

Thanks to the Boldheart community and our intrepid leader Fabienne Fredrickson, for encouraging me to get this book out into the world, and to Paulette Perhach in particular. That bitch contains multitudes.

Thank you to my extended family: Bill Collier, Carla Keefer, Juan Dávila, Liz Dávila, Summer Bradley, Ollie Bradley, Tallulah Bradley, Otis Bradley, Sarah Hughes (the cousin who belly flopped on my sandcastles), Becky Santos, Catherine Dávila, Matt Gulley, and especially my wonderfully talented mom, Michele Collier, who created the final illustrations for this book. (Mom, I know I mentioned Dad three times in this book, and you maybe felt left out, but those mentions were mostly in relation to trauma, so I hope you will see the fact that I didn't include you as a compliment. Thanks for creating a stable, loving, safe home for me to grow up in.)

To Cassie Gruenstein, Syd Richards, Katie Pollard, and Anne Leache: Thanks for all the hilarious texts; they keep me going. You're all too far away, but always in my heart. And to my local ladies: Adrienne Alitowski, Pearlin De Long, Elisa Parhad, Susan Littenberg, Carmen Balber, Brenda Carmona. More coffee dates, please.

For my kind, thoughtful, hilarious children, Celeste and Sebastian, who have taught me so much about approaching the world with openhearted curiosity. I love you both more than words could possibly say.

For Daniel, my love, my everything. Thank you for your unending patience and enthusiasm, for your creative ideas and insightful feedback. I simply could not do this without you.

# ABOUT THE AUTHOR

**April Dávila** is an award-winning author, speaker, and writing coach. *Publishers Weekly* called her debut novel, *142 Ostriches*, a "vivid, uplifting debut" and the book went on to win the WILLA Award for Women Writing the West. *Writer's Digest* listed her blog (at aprildavila.com) as one of the Best 101 Websites for Writers, and she is the creator of the Sit Write Here writing and coaching program, helping writers quiet their inner critics, overcome writer's block, and edit more effectively.